Children's
Mental Health Matters

Copyright © 2025 by Cassie Swift et al

All rights reserved.

No portion of this book may be reproduced in any form without written permission from the publisher or author, except as permitted by UK copyright law.

This publication is designed to provide accurate and authoritative information in regard to the subject matter covered. It is sold with the understanding that neither the author nor the publisher is engaged in rendering legal, investment, accounting or other professional services. While the publisher and author have used their best efforts in preparing this book, they make no representations or warranties with respect to the accuracy or completeness of the contents of this book and specifically disclaim any implied warranties of merchantability or fitness for a particular purpose. No warranty may be created or extended by sales representatives or written sales materials. The advice and strategies contained herein may not be suitable for your situation. You should consult with a professional when appropriate. Neither the publisher nor the author shall be liable for any loss of profit or any other commercial damages, including but not limited to special, incidental, consequential, personal, or other damages.

ISBN number for this book: 978-1-7396179-5-0

Cover design by Heather Hulbert, www.heatherhulbert.co.uk

Disclaimer

Please be aware that this book contains topics of a sensitive nature, some of which people may find upsetting or triggering. For permissions, contact cassie@childrensmentalhealthmatters.co.uk

This book is not intended to be a comprehensive medical guide. The opinions and information expressed in this publication are those of the authors only, and they are sharing their expertise but do not represent professional advice. This book is not intended as a substitute for seeking professional medical advice, and the reader should regularly consult a medical expert in matters relating to their health, particularly with respect to any symptoms that might require a diagnosis or medical attention. The authors take no responsibility for any actions taken as a result of reading this book and do not assume and hereby disclaim any liability for any losses occurring as a result.

Trigger warning: please be advised that this book talks about issues which may be triggering, including high-conflict divorce, eating disorders, self-harm, and illness.

Contents

1. Introduction — 1
2. Let's Talk About Self-Harm — 3
   By Cassie Swift
3. 'You said we had lost Granny, can we go and look for her?' — 21
   How to support a child dealing with bereavement, loss, and grief By Sara Bowater
4. The Benefits of Co-regulation — 35
   By Sarah Burnett
5. Self-Care when Caring for Mental Health — 49
   By Duncan Casburn
6. The Power of Breath — 59
   Supporting Your Child's Physical, Mental, and Emotional Wellbeing By Fleur Conway
7. When School Feels Impossible — 73
   Understanding Autistic Burnout, Emotionally-Based School Avoidance, and the Restorative Magic of Hypno-Stories By Amy Dalwood-Fairbanks

8.	Nature's Classroom Nurturing Resilience, Confidence, and Creativity Outdoors By Lucy Fenwick	87
9.	Putting Children First Reducing the Harm of High-Conflict Divorce By AJ Gajjar	97
10.	Why Food Matters in Mental Health By Lucy Harper	109
11.	Nurturing Hearts Meeting the Emotional Needs of Your Child By Keri Hartwright	121
12.	Compliance to Confidence Nurturing Autonomy and Intrinsic Motivation Protects Young People's Wellbeing By Laura Linklater	133
13.	The Journey of Understanding and Being Empowered from Behind the Mask of Neurodiversity, Eating Disorders, Mental Health, Suicide, Self-Harm, Trauma, and Other Life Experiences By Emily Nuttall	147
14.	Mental Health and Migration By Jules Reynolds	161
15.	Exploring Neurodiversity for Your Child By Emma Sails	173
Other Collaborative Projects By Cassie Swift		187

Introduction

If you have picked up this book, I am going to assume that your child or a young person you know is struggling with their mental health. I see you, and you are not alone.

The aim of this book is to provide information, strategies, and advice on a range of different mental health issues which many young people today may be experiencing. I hope that it will be helpful for you and bring some hope to your situation.

If you need any further support, please reach out to any of the authors whose contact details can be found at the end of each chapter via a link, or any of the charities listed throughout the book.

At the beginning of each individual chapter, you will also find a QR code which will provide you with an audio version of each chapter read by the author.

This book is dedicated to all the children, young people, parents and caregivers out there trying to navigate the many systems associated with the world we currently live in and to overcome the many obstacles we are faced with.

You are not alone; we see you, and there is help out there. Always hold onto hope, and the glimmer of light will appear.

Let's Talk About Self-Harm
By Cassie Swift

'Even the darkest night will end, and the sun will rise.' — *Victor Hugo*

As I am going to be covering the subject of self-harm, I will place an additional Content Warning here, as some things I discuss may be upsetting or act as a 'trigger' for some people. If this happens, please do seek help by contacting myself or other charities I mention towards the end of this chapter.

I also want to state that I am not medically trained; the information included here is a result of training and research, as well as actual lived experience. I have lived this journey, so please know that it is possible to come out the other side. I am reluctant to use the word 'recover', as I feel some thoughts will always remain during extremely challenging times; however, it is the way we approach the situation that will change.

What is Self-Harm?

Let us begin by defining and clarifying exactly what self-harm is. The charity MIND defines it as, 'when you hurt yourself as a way of dealing with very difficult feelings, painful memories, or overwhelming situations and experiences'. I would like to add that it also includes any action or behaviour used to intentionally hurt yourself.

Some other terms or abbreviations that you may come across are SI (Self Injury,) NSSI (Non-Suicidal Self Injury), or SM (Self-Mutilation).

Self-harm is becoming spoken about much more. However, sometimes people will avoid talking about self-harm at all and this can be for several reasons, including societal stigma; not wanting to use the term self-harm; trying to play it down or almost 'sugarcoat it' due to its connotations; and also judgement — or should I say the fear of judgement — feeling like you have failed as a person, parent, or caregiver. There is also the fear of what might happen if it is spoken about, perhaps a referral to social services and their involvement. But these are just a couple of examples.

The Self-Harm Cycle

When I talk about self-harm, I often refer to the self-harm cycle, which you can see below:

Let me explain in more detail. Self-harm usually starts with 'emotional suffering', and by that I mean emotions that lie beneath the surface which the child or young person cannot regulate, whether this be anxiety, depression, grief, sadness, or whatever. The child or young person suppresses it and pushes it down so that they don't have to deal with it. But it bubbles away under the surface until we hit 'emotional overwhelm' — when something (it could be a 'big' event or one that society deems as 'small') happens that just tips the person over. This could be anything at all, like a fall-out with someone, a test at school, or even a drawing not turning out as envisioned — literally anything. Think of what happens when you add Mentos to Coke (the Coke explodes out of the bottle), or the saying 'the straw that broke the camel's back'.

This leads to complete dysregulation and 'panic' — a panic that cannot be pushed back down, and as a result the act of self-harm can occur to try and claim back some control or to find some relief from this overbearing feeling. The act of self-harm can provide a TEMPORARY relief of the panic and overwhelm due to the 'dopamine hit' that it provides.

However, this does not last long and is soon followed by feelings of guilt, shame, and failure, which leads back into the underlying emotional suffering. So, the cycle begins again and continues round and round. For this reason, a person won't simply 'grow out of it', because it becomes addictive; that feeling of relief — no matter how temporary — becomes sought after. And the longer it continues, the more severe the self-harm can become, in the same way an alcoholic will increase the amount of alcohol drunk to hit that same feeling.

Let's do some 'myth-busting'

At this point I want to address some 'myths' you may have heard about self-harm.

1. 'It is just attention seeking' — Normally, those who self-harm do it in places that cannot be seen (upper arms, thighs, torso). IF, however, they begin doing it in more visible places. it is likely that they want help, but due to shame, guilt, or embarrassment they don't know how to actually verbalise and ask for help. By doing it where someone will see it, they are taking a risk and being vulnerable. This is your chance to open a conversation, rather than brushing it off and saying it is 'attention seeking' or ignoring it altogether.

2. 'They will grow out of it' — They will not and cannot simply grow out of it. As I have already discussed with the Self-Harm Cycle, the behaviour becomes an addiction.

3. 'It's the latest craze' or 'all their friends are doing it' — I

am not saying that no-one will 'try' self-harm because it is what they have seen or heard others doing. However, if it is done more than once, it isn't because of this. Remember, self-harm hurts! So, if it isn't a serious issue that requires help, no-one would do it more than once just for 'fun'.

4. 'They are suicidal' — Self-harm is not a sign someone wants to end their life; it is a sign of deep emotional distress. Self-harm is a risk factor and so should be monitored on an individual basis, of course. But self-harming in itself does not mean that someone is suicidal.

5. 'They are dangerous/violent' — I want to caveat this and say that there may be some people who are, and you know your child or young person better than anyone else, so again take this on an individual basis. The majority of those who self-harm, though, are not dangerous or violent. They would much rather take their feelings out on themselves than others, which is why they self-harm.

I am sure there are many other things that you have heard that I have not covered here, but these are the most common.

Why does someone self-harm?

There are many reasons why someone may self-harm, but below is a list of the most common reasons:

- Anxiety and depression

- Unable to identify or verbalise emotions

- The need to have some control over their life

- Overarching feeling of self-loathing

- Abuse (mental, physical, emotional, sexual)

- Grief

- Bullying

- School needs not being met (whether through SEN (Special educational Needs) or EBSA (Emotional Based School Avoidance))

- Academic pressure

- Sexuality (The LGBTQIA+ community are higher risk)

- The only way to actually feel. Some people become so dissociated (or separated) from themselves and their reality that they become completely numb, and self-harm is the only way in which they can physically feel anything.

Ways in which someone may self-harm

There are also many ways in which someone can self-harm — some obvious, others that may be new to you. Again, this list is not exhaustive in any way, but will hopefully provide a good insight:

- Cutting (commonly used are razors and knives, but sometimes pencil sharpeners and compasses; if someone is desperate enough, even broken glass)

- Burning

- Punching themselves or walls/doors

- Banging their head

- Pulling their hair out

- Scratching repetitively in one place until it becomes sore or bleeds

- Ingesting poisonous substances. If this happens, visit or phone the emergency department at your nearest hospital and do not induce vomiting (unless directed to do so by a medical professional).

- Drinking alcohol in large amounts and regularly

- Taking drugs

- Having unsafe sex

- Putting themselves at risk, for example, going out late at night without telling anyone

- Over-exercising

- Controlling food/eating disorders (see below a brief summary of the many different eating disorders there are:

    - Anorexia — when someone restricts food completely and starves themselves

    - Bulimia — when someone binges (eating large quantities or food) and then purges (makes themselves sick)

- Binge Eating Disorder — Bingeing without purging

- ARFID (Avoidant Restrictive Food Intake Disorder) — the person avoids certain foods or certain types of food, restricting what they eat

- Rumination — this is rare, but it is when someone brings food back up from their stomach and either rechews, swallows, or spits it out

- Pica — when someone eats non-food items with no nutritional value, such as paper, toilet tissue, paint, chalk, or ice, to name a few

- OSFED (Other Specified Feeding or Eating Disorder) — when someone may have symptoms that are similar to one or more eating disorders but does not fulfil the full criteria for a diagnosis

If you suspect any of these food/eating disorders, please contact your local GP. You can also visit the website BEAT, which is a specialist eating disorder charity in the UK:

https://www.beateatingdisorders.org.uk or NEDA in the USA: https://www.nationaleatingdisorders.org. You can Google 'Eating Disorder Charities in... (and enter your country)' to find support in your area.

Signs that your child or young person is self-harming

How do you know if your child or young person may be self-harming?

There are many signs that you can look out for — again, some more obvious than others. For example:

- Unexplained cuts, bruises, or cigarette burns, usually on the upper arms, thighs, and chest, sometimes wrists and lower arms

- Keeping themselves fully covered even in hot weather; wearing a long-sleeved top in the height of summer is a big sign, or not going swimming due to not wanting to wear a costume/shorts

- Bald patches

- Self-loathing and expressing a wish to 'punish' themselves in some way

- Becoming very withdrawn and not speaking to others

- Signs of low self-esteem or depression, e.g. again withdrawal, poor hygiene, negative self-talk

- Unusual weight fluctuations

- Food going missing from cupboards — this could be an indicator to bingeing behaviour

- Changes in eating habits or being secretive about eating

- Visiting the bathroom soon after eating a meal — this could be an indicator that they are making themselves sick

- Being obsessed with exercise and doing more than previously

Again, this is not an exhaustive list but gives an idea of things to look out for.

What do I do if I suspect or find out my child or young person is self-harming?

Firstly, and this is a difficult one: DO NOT PANIC! Please take some time to compose yourself before doing anything. I know this is a highly emotive situation, but in order for your child to trust you, you have to remain calm. If they have told you, it has taken a lot of courage to do so, and they probably already feel embarrassed, guilty, and ashamed, so they need a safe space. So, please try not to shout, cry, or panic in front of them — even if this means you tell them you need a few moments to process what they have told you, and it isn't their fault but just you regulating your own emotions. This also shows them that there are other ways to deal with emotions.

If you discover or suspect they have self-harmed, but they haven't told you, again try to remain as calm as possible and ask them, 'Have you self-harmed?' You will know instantly by their reaction whether they have or not. I want to add here that simply asking them will not make them start self-harming if they haven't already, so please don't be afraid to ask.

Next, do NOT start removing and locking everything away. Remember, as I said earlier, often self-harm occurs when they feel they have no control over their life. If you take everything away, they will still find something, whether it is broken glass or a rusty nail — and what that does is increase the risk of infection. So, while I know it goes against everything you believe, letting them have access to something that is sterile will decrease the risk of infection. If you want to put everything away, I understand, but talk to them and tell them they can access something sterile, for example, a new razor. The truth is that unfortunately self-harming cannot just be stopped overnight, so you have to find a way of working together.

Then, make sure you have a fully equipped First Aid kit, including burn coverings, skin closure strips, and saline (a sterile liquid solution containing salt and water which helps clean wounds thoroughly). If nothing else, ensuring that wounds are clean and covered to avoid infection is of paramount importance! Teaching your child how to look after their wounds is one of the most important things you can do at the start of this journey, and it will demonstrate to them that you care, you are meeting them where they are, and you will journey through it together.

Emotions take ninety seconds to heighten before they begin to fall again and allow for rational thinking. Therefore, if they can learn to distract themselves for this time, the risk of self-harming will decrease rapidly. I always recommend EFT (Emotional Freedom Technique — also known as tapping) for this, as it calms the nervous system down and enables the rational/logical part of the brain to work again much quicker. So, if they can tap on their collarbones for ninety seconds, this will help. If they are able to control their breath using 'rectangle breathing' (described below), it will also significantly bring down the urge to self-harm.

Rectangle breathing is when you draw a rectangle in your mind, you breathe in as you make the shorter side of the rectangle, and breathe out for the longer side, then repeat again to finish the rectangle. Doing this two or three times will help calm your body down, as making the outbreath longer than the inbreath signals to your body that you are safe and allows you to relax.

You may have heard of other ways to provide distractions, and whilst I am not completely discounting them, I have found through experience and that of others that they can be counterintuitive. Some examples are pinging an elastic band on your wrist, holding an ice cube, or drawing on yourself with a red pen. The problem is these all feed into the self-harm mindset and can hurt in some way but not quite enough. This can then lead to frustration and exacerbate the desire to self-harm, resulting in the behaviour anyway. So, I would approach these ways with caution.

I want to add an aside here. If the result of self-harm is significant, please take the young person to the hospital emergency department to seek medical help. Beforehand, it may be helpful to speak to them about medical terms they might hear. The most common will be 'superficial wound', and this phrase can be highly triggering, indicating in some way that the wound isn't bad enough. This might make the person feel like they haven't 'self-harmed properly' or they are 'wasting the hospital's time', again feeding into those feelings of worthlessness and embarrassment.

In medical terms, the word 'superficial' describes something very different; it is the medical term for how deep a cut is. So, if a cut goes through the top layer of skin (epidermis) or slightly into the second layer (dermis), it is classed as 'superficial'. It will undoubtedly need some kind of stitches, but it means it isn't near to the muscle or bone. Take time to assure them that it doesn't mean it isn't serious, but it is just how medical professionals communicate between themselves so they know what they are dealing with.

Techniques to help

There are several techniques which can help with the urge of self-harm, including:

- EFT (tapping)

- Going for a walk

- Standing barefoot on the ground to help your body regulate

- Taking a bath or shower

- Listening to music

- Dancing or going for a run (if exercise is not an issue)

- Journaling

- Colouring or drawing

- And, if open to it, meditation and breathing techniques, such as the rectangle breathing described earlier

Alternatively, and I strongly recommend this, is creating what I term a 'Box of Hope'™, sometimes called distraction boxes or self-soothe boxes (it doesn't have to be a box; it can be a container of any sort; or even a bag or pouch). The idea is that they build the contents of this box and put things in it, giving it a personal meaning as well as providing a variety of distraction tools.

Below is a list of some ideas, but the point is to make it personal and filled with things that they will find helpful and bring them hope and some joy:

- Photos of family, friends, pets, holidays

- USB with favourite songs, hymns, background sounds (an online playlist could also be created for this purpose)

- Fidget toys

- Lego

- Small puzzles

- Nail varnish

- Hand cream
- Essential oils
- Battery-operated candles
- Comforting perfume
- Favourite chocolate bar (if food isn't an issue)
- Popping candy
- Bottle of water (this can help regulate breathing)
- Journal
- Drawing pad
- Mindful colouring
- Pens (I wouldn't recommend pencils, as you don't want to put things like pencil sharpeners in there)
- Affirmations
- Breathing techniques
- Letters or cards from other people
- Emergency phone number list
- Anything else which is special to them. I would avoid anything that needs a lighter or pencil sharpener, or anything that could cause harm.

I know I have packed in a lot of information, so please go back and reread the parts that are relevant to you.

If you are going through this, I know how difficult it is, but please try to be kind to yourself as well as your child, and do not be afraid to ask for help. There are people and organisations that can help. Also remember there is no quick fix; it is a journey that you need to go on together whilst also allowing each other space. Connection is vitally important throughout, opening up about feelings and emotions, which might not always be by speaking to one another. Many teens find it difficult to talk, so you could try writing in a notebook to one another, or even texting/messaging one another, to avoid putting extra pressure on them. And finally, please know you are NOT ALONE; you will need support, too, so reach out to friends, families, or organisations. And never give up hope — there is light at the end of the tunnel, no matter how long the journey is to get there.

If you have any questions, feel free to contact me via the link in my biography. Alternatively, there are charities that can help, I have mentioned ones relating to eating disorders, but there is also Young Minds: https://www.youngminds.org.uk and MIND: https://www.mind.org.uk and Battle Scars: https://www.battle-scars-self-harm.org.ukalong with many others which you can find online.

Dedication:

I dedicate this chapter to my younger self who has given me this wisdom to be able to help others. I also dedicate this to all those on this journey. I see you and know you too will make it through and go on to help others in ways you cannot yet see!

Biography:

Cassie has been described by her children as 'awesome, kind, incredible, caring, beautiful, and AMAZEBALLS'. A single mother of three, her friends describe her as a kind-hearted, loving, and courageous woman who will stand up for her beliefs and the rights of others. Cassie experienced bullying throughout her entire school life and wishes she'd had someone to turn to, because her mental health deteriorated as a result. This is not something anyone would wish for a child, and no-one deserves to feel this way or experience what she went through.

Cassie works as a Family Empowerment Guide, specifically with teens, to enable them to feel empowered about life. She helps them to manage big emotions in a positive way, accepting the true version of themselves. As a result, she brings calm and happiness not only to those she works with, but to the whole family. She is trained in several holistic approaches, including NLP, EFT, Hypnotherapy, and EFT specifically for teens, as well as a lot of life experience which helps to put her unique spin on things.

Cassie is also a #1 Best Selling Author of eight books, three of which she co-created, as well as the founder and organiser of the Children's Mental Health Matters Summit. She has featured on the radio and in six local newspapers, speaking about issues surrounding Children's Mental Health.

She explains, 'Helping others, especially children, is my passion. I want to empower as many children as I possibly can!'

You can connect with Cassie here:

https://linktr.ee/CassieS

'You said we had lost Granny, can we go and look for her?'

How to support a child dealing with bereavement, loss, and grief By Sara Bowater

'Sometimes the healing hurts more than the wound.' Unknown[1]

As a teacher, and Head of House/pastoral lead for approximately 220 11-18-year-olds, my heart would sink when I received a call or email to say that one of my pupils had suffered a bereavement or was dealing with the separation of parents. For years I felt I was doing my

---

1. https://www.cruse.org.uk/about/blog/blog-grief-quotes/

best, but none of us are ever taught how to deal with the difficulties in life; there is no guidebook, there is no teacher training about these issues, so we all bumble along hoping for the best. We see those we love and care for hurting, and we are unable to assess if we are adequately supporting them.

Like others, I have had my fair share of loss and grief over the years. Between the ages of 14 to 25, I was bullied at school, then dealt with losing most of my immediate family, including the sudden death of my father at the airport and the suicide of my godmother. Even though the rest of the family tried to support me, they were all dealing with their own grief. I left home and went to university, was diagnosed as dyslexic, but I dealt with all of my feelings on my own as I was under the impression that was what I needed to do.

During this time, I received two very different levels of support — virtually nothing from my secondary school, bar a quick chat with my Head of Year, but a really structured support programme from my university tutors (something that I will be eternally thankful for). My experiences highlighted to me that no-one really knows what to do or what to say, and the condescending comment of 'everyone goes through it' does not help.

Knowing that grief and loss are inevitable, I did not want my students to suffer alone; I wanted something tangible to do with them to stop any loss being something that defined them. About eight years ago I came across the Grief Recovery Method® and its *Helping Children with Loss* programme. It is no exaggeration to say that it changed my life personally and professionally, but especially the way I now support my pupils. It provided me with a new skillset, new language, and a different set of lenses to see grief and loss through. I learnt what to do, what not to do, and how grief is unique to each and every one of us.

So, what is grief?

The Grief Recovery Method® defines grief as 'a normal and natural reaction to loss', and a loss is 'a change in normal pattern of behaviour'.[2] When we look at grief in this way, we suddenly see that a significant number of losses or change of events that happen to us in our everyday lives can now be classed as events that create feelings of grief. For me, this was a lightbulb moment. I realised that the behaviour I was seeing in the classroom was a result of loss — and lots of different types of losses; not just from children who had suffered a bereavement or were dealing with parental separation. I became more aware of the child who was being bullied (and had lost their feelings of security), or the child who had recently been diagnosed with an SEND need, or the child whose pet had just died. They too were grieving and needed to be heard and supported.

Our job (as the adults) is to listen and ask the right questions so that we can look deeper to find the root causes of changes in behaviour and, ultimately, to help our young people successfully navigate life. Rather than seeing just the behaviour exhibited (and labelling that behaviour), we should explore further to find out what is going on in their lives and what has caused them to behave in this way. As Devina

---

2. John W. James and Russell Friedman, *The Grief Recovery Handbook, 20th Anniversary Expanded Edition: The Action Program for Moving Beyond Death, Divorce, and Other Losses including Health, Career, and Faith*– Dec 2017, William Marrow Paperbacks.

King says, 'Every form of behaviour is a form of communication — it is up to us to decipher it.'[3]

Our children are unlikely to have the skills or language to adequately explain their feelings and emotions, so most of our young people are desperate to be heard and listened to without being judged or criticised. But they just don't know how to ask for this support. I have always believed that the way a child behaves is their way of trying to express themselves, and they need to be properly heard to start to feel better and be given the right tools to support themselves. One of my pieces of advice would be to look at how a child is presenting and look for deeper root causes — most of the time it will be a loss where grief has been left unresolved or not listened to.

It is estimated that a child can experience over 15 types of losses before they reach the age of 16, while an adult can experience over 40 different types of losses during their lives.[4] Some of the most obvious loss events include:

- Divorce or separation of partners

- Death of a child, parent, sibling, close family member, or friend

- Death of a pet

- Illness that is life-changing or life-limiting

- Moving house, school, class, or job

---

3. Devina King, *Surviving To Thriving: The Art and Science of Guiding Children To Develop Behavioural Regulation* – Feb 2024, Amazon Kindle Edition

4. https://www.griefrecoverymethod.com/blog/2021/01/change-comes-grief-over-40-life-events-cause-heartache

- Being made redundant

- Being a looked-after child

- Being abused

We only need to listen to the news to be aware of the growing mental crisis of our young people which schools and agencies are struggling to deal with. As parents, educators, or professionals working with young people, the news and statistics paint a very depressing landscape that our young people live in. To provide a flavour:

- 127 children are bereaved of a parent every day in the UK.[5] 1 in 20 children and young people have experienced the death of a parent by the age of 16 — that's at least one in every classroom.[6]

- The NSPCC notes that 'In 2022/23, there were approximately 107,000 looked-after children in the UK. In the last five years the population of looked-after children in the UK has increased by 8%.'[7]

- In 2023 there were 2.4 million families separated in Great Britain, with 3.8 million children in those separated

---

5. https://harrysrainbow.co.uk/national-stats

6. https://www.winstonswish.org/about-us/facts-and-figures/

7. https://learning.nspcc.org.uk/research-resources/statistics-briefings/looked-after-children

8. https://www.gov.uk/government/statistics/separated-families-statistics-april-2014-to-march-2023/separated-families-statistics-april-2014-to-march-2023

families [8]

Many of our young people are dealing with trauma caused by a number of Adverse Childhood Experiences (or ACEs), e.g. death of a parent, abuse, living with someone who is a drug addict or alcoholic. Some of our children may be dealing with one ACE but many will be handling multiple ACEs at the same time. These statistics are just the tip of the iceberg, and most of us are at a loss on how to support them. Imagine a child has a rucksack, and with every loss they face they add a stone to their rucksack. It is not going to take long before that child is carrying a huge burden. They often do not have any useful strategies to help them deal with their losses or the weight of emotions they are carrying. So, they will often turn to carrying out unhealthy behaviours to help them deal with and process the losses and emotions they feel.

Everyone is STERBing

Educational psychologists noted that our brains do not fully develop until our mid-20s. The pre-frontal cortex, which deals with planning, helps us make good decisions, and more importantly deals with our emotions, is the last to mature. This part of the brain also deals with our working memory and helps us understand and react to others' emotions.

Society tends to shy away from talking about emotions, so our young people are never taught how to process these or to deal with sadness and hurt. We are encouraged to feel happy, but we are often explicitly (and implicitly) told not to be sad or unhappy. Children will often follow their elders and copy their coping strategies, e.g. crying on their own, drinking to numb the pain felt, etc. These coping strategies help us process how we feel, to some extent.

So, what does a child do when they feel they can't express their negative emotions to anyone? They swallow them or bottle them up, like we do. They create these emotional furballs because they have no skills to deal with how they feel. They start to act differently — possibly in a challenging manner; they are angry or isolated from others; they turn to unhealthy behaviours to mask the pain they feel; and they act up.

The Grief Recovery Method® calls these behaviours STERBs, or Short-Term Energy-Relieving Behaviours.[9] When we STERB we produce a short-term positive feeling that gives us the impression that we have dealt with our emotions. But when we come down from this positive feeling, we often feel very low and realise the situation has not changed; STERBs give us the illusion that momentarily we have dealt with our loss. STERBs act as a mechanism to allow some of the stored emotional energy to be released. Like a pressure cooker, if the valve does not work, the cooker will explode. If we don't get rid of some of the trapped energy, a person will often have an emotional breakdown.

STERBs are necessary, but they need to be managed. We need to be aware of them, aware of the STERBs we carry out, and also the STERBs our children carry out. Knowing your child well, and noticing their change of habits and behaviours, will help you identify when they are STERBing and help you to find out the root cause.

---

9. John W James and Russell Friedman, *The Grief Recovery Handbook, 20th Anniversary Expanded Edition: The Action Program for Moving Beyond Death, Divorce, and Other Losses including Health, Career, and Faith*– Dec 2017, William Marrow Paperbacks.

Time to re-educate our thoughts

Social media and media provide us with advice on how to deal with emotions. The only issue is that most of the information we pass on is not helpful. The Grief Recovery Method® identifies six myths or pieces of misinformation that is shared from generation to generation, with each generation not questioning or checking whether the information or advice is helpful and relevant.

1. Don't feel sad

2. Replace the loss

3. Grieve alone

4. Be strong for others

5. Time heals

6. Keep busy

Those who embark on any of the Grief Recovery Method's® programmes, especially the *Helping Children with Loss* course, will learn more about these myths or misconceptions and the impact they have on us as adults, but especially the messages our children receive. In most cases these are thoughts/phrases/sayings, etc, that cause the griever to minimise their loss, make them feel that they cannot be listened to or heard, and stop them from processing how they feel. Our young people will watch and hear things via the media and social media that reinforce these messages.

Most of the comments used — e.g. 'Man up!', 'You are now the man of the house', 'They are no longer suffering', 'They are in a better place', 'There are plenty more fish in the sea', or 'It's been three years since their grandma died' — are phrases we hear all the time. But have we ever stopped to consider the impact they have on us, or whether they are actually useful? Probably not. These myths often cause us to intellectualise grief so that it becomes something we need to rationally think about rather than dealing with the emotions we have. If we focus on how we feel and allow our hearts to do the talking, we can process a loss event a little easier.

In most cases the emotional feelings we have are linked to unresolved grief; things we have not had a chance to say or do, or wish we hadn't done, or had done differently, or where our dreams/hopes and aspirations have not been fulfilled or met. This will be the same for positive and negative relationships. These myths do not allow us to deal with these feelings of unresolved grief; rather, we bottle them up and carry them with us. We use and pass on the misconceptions to our children, having never questioned why they are used. Don't get annoyed with yourself if you are suddenly aware of what you have been saying. We have all said them; especially me! Now try to consider what you are saying and whether the advice is useful.

Sara's Top Tips

Being emotionally honest with your children is really important. They look to us to help them navigate their way through life; they follow and copy what we do and say. If your child does not see you being emotionally honest or crying openly, they may feel that they should do the same and grieve on their own. This often results in them not sharing or showing how they feel and finding other ways to express their emotions. ELSAs (Emotional Literacy Support Assistants) and teachers will often use feelings cards to help a child to verbally describe their emotions. Model being emotionally honest every day, and when a child needs to share how they feel, they will already have the language and understanding to do so — and, more importantly, feel safe to do so.

We all need to be heard; really heard. So, practise actively listening and being in the moment. Give your child your full attention when they talk to you, especially if they are sharing how they feel. Look them in the eye and provide lots of non-verbal reassurances that encourage them to continue sharing their feelings. This will take time to practise and is hard to do. Active listening also means not interrupting someone sharing their story or thoughts. I have been known to sit on my hands to stop myself interrupting, but listening to someone means allowing them to speak, not filling the awkward silences, or adding our own experiences to their story.

Think about the language you use to describe a loss. I purposely chose the title of this chapter as it centres around a child's literal understanding of a phrase we often use when someone has died —'we have lost them'. But children take our language quite literally. For example, saying that you have 'lost Granny' rather than saying 'Granny has died' can lead some children to physically start to look for Granny and ask to go and find her. Saying that Sparkle the goldfish 'has gone to sleep' can cause some children to worry about going to sleep and not waking up. Use the D words of death and died and the F word being funeral. Being factually honest, whilst hard, will help a child in the long run.

When there is a loss event that can be planned for, e.g. moving schools, moving house, or even the death of someone, allow a child to say their goodbyes and be allowed to express how they feel. Allow their feelings to be heard, as even a positive change can bring feelings of loss. It might be nice to create a memory box where the child can add items, such as photos, cards, or objects that remind them of what they may be about to lose. It can provide a tangible reminder of their past experiences and allows them to hold onto cherished memories. They can open this box whenever they need to and add things to it over time, as this often provides comfort.

Creating a memory box after a sudden loss event is also wise. I created one after my dad died, and I love to take out the letters he wrote to me at university and wear his signet ring; they provide a feeling of him being close. Another way of holding onto cherished memories is by creating a memory paper chain. Here a memory is described on the piece of paper and links are made. These can be used to decorate a bedroom or special place whilst also be added to as often as a cherished memory surfaces. Both memory boxes and paper chains also allow for deep meaningful reflection conversations which help our young people connect with the past but also share some of their trapped emotions.

My best piece of advice would be to normalise grief and loss as much as possible. It is nothing to shy away from but rather to see these events as normal and natural parts of life. By allowing a child to grieve and helping them through the difficult times, you help them to be more resilient in the future. Look for moments that help them to learn to grieve. For example, if a pet dies, don't rush out to replace it. Allow a child to grieve and talk about the pet. Explain that the feelings they have are normal and natural. Talk about how they may want to remember their pet or whether they want some sort of funeral service.

Final Thoughts

There is not adequate space to condense everything I have learnt over the years, but I hope the ideas and experiences shared provide some guidance. You are not alone. The more we talk about grief, the easier it will be to support our young people.

Dedication:

This chapter is dedicated to the children I have supported through grief and loss. Your courage and bravery are always an inspiration. Your sorrow was the catalyst to find something that helped you to rediscover your potential and to stop you from being defined by the challenges you faced. I hope in some small way the support I have offered has provided some light in the darkest of your days. You deserve so much, and you have the potential to change the world in which we live. Believe in yourself and use the skills you have been taught. Nothing is impossible.

I would also like to dedicate this chapter to all the Grief Recovery Specialists who are helping and supporting so many people to recover from the grief they are facing. John James, and his Grief Recovery Method®, has changed my life, and I will be eternally thankful to him and Russell Friedman. I thank Cole, Ed, Lois, and Susan for being wonderful mentors. Thank you, Catherine, for training me and always being there when I needed you; you are an inspirational lady, and I can never thank you enough. You, Sarah, and Dinah are my Grief Recovery family; you mean the world to me. Thank you for believing in me each and every day, as well as sharing the same mission as me to get Grief Recovery's Helping Children with Loss course into every school so that more children can be supported.

Dad is always in my heart and continues to be the wind behind my wings, even though I physically cannot be with him. This chapter is dedicated to him and my family, especially my husband Nige.

Biography:

Sara Bowater has over 25 years' experience of teaching and supporting children at both primary and secondary level in the United Kingdom. She trained and taught as a primary teacher before moving into a secondary school. She has been a Head of Department but has spent the last 11 years at the heart of pastoral support, as well as being a Deputy Designated Safeguarding Lead. As a Head of House, she had responsibility for the pastoral and academic development of 220 11-18-year-olds.

In 2019 she trained as a Grief Recovery specialist with the Grief Recovery Institute before becoming an Advanced Grief Recovery Specialist in 2020. She was a joint author of the Grief Recovery Institute's *Online Helping Children with Loss* programme and was a contributing writer to Grief UK's *Open Ears* programme. She regularly runs *Helping Children with Loss* courses and also supports adults on a 1-1 basis via an eight-week programme.

Sara is passionate about the support young children experience around loss and would dearly love to change the narrative and experiences that children receive.

You can connect with Sara here:

https://linktr.ee/sarabowaterbickmore

The Benefits of Co-regulation
By Sarah Burnett

'You may not control all the events that happen to you, but you can decide not to be reduced by them.' Maya Angelou, Letter to My Daughter

Imagine this...

You are walking along a quiet road, the weather is exactly how you like it to be, the sounds around you bringing a sense of calm, there's a comforting smell in the air, and you have your favourite clothes on. Maybe you can smell a pleasant waft of cooking coming from a nearby house, and any pain you might usually experience seems to be in the background for a change. All is well with the world, and you have a sense of hopeful anticipation. Suddenly a massive lorry comes hurtling out of nowhere towards you, and you jump out of the way to safety. What are you feeling in your body now? A typical nervous system working at optimal level will feel the effects of adrenaline and everything that goes with a fight and flight response. Then, after the danger has passed, it will return to its previous state, although maybe not quite as relaxed as before.

Now, imagine that your nervous system isn't working at optimal level and that it doesn't return to its ideal state. How might that feel? What if that's the state you had to function in for the rest of your life? The reality is that this is the case for some people, especially those who receive more sensory input from the world than most, unless they can find a way to calm and regulate their system before reintroducing it to appropriate (specifically to them) levels of challenge. That's where co-regulation (bringing a felt sense of safety to help another also achieve a sense of safety) comes in.

Learning how to regulate ourselves is potentially the most powerful thing we can do for our children. And I know from first-hand experience just how important 'safe' people are when your nervous system has become 'stuck' for some reason. Meeting someone's needs is not enabling, spoiling, or pandering to them; it is allowing them a chance to heal and reset so they can take on more if and when they are ready.

For many parents, especially those with chronic health challenges, chronically stressful circumstances, and dependants with significant needs outside of the 'norm', accessing a regulated state can be a real challenge. Not only can we not find time to help ourselves, but often the things we need to do to help us and our children are counter-cultural and go against deeply ingrained beliefs and values. It's hard. So, if this is you, I assure you that there is hope and that with small steps we can create big changes. Additionally, when our children see us using healthy strategies to deal with challenging circumstances, they can learn to value their own self-care, too.

A caveat

I must caveat this with two opposites. Some don't have the 'luxury' of exploring and learning new things potentially needed to regulate their nervous systems in the circumstances they're in. They just need someone to listen, believe their experience, and support them. Others may find we don't have the 'luxury' of not exploring and learning how to (I mean those of us who experience a complete malfunction and can't function as a result). We are not all experiencing the same thing, we all have different starting points, and we are all shaped by a variety of experiences — some supportive, some not so much. With this in mind, please take what is helpful and leave the rest, knowing that not everything speaks to all situations. There will be a unique way for you, and I hope you find it.

I am not a mental health 'expert'. However, I do have a long history of chronic health challenges, have navigated my own nervous system recovery, and have used co-regulation as a part of parenting for longer than I understood what I was doing — as many of us do. For the most part, co-regulation is automatic; we're designed to do it, and many don't even need to consider it. However, when we have a family member (possibly including us) who experiences significant nervous system dysregulation symptoms, for whatever reason, consciously learning about co-regulation and rapport (coming alongside each other in trust and mutual understanding) can become life-changing for all involved.

This has been the case for my family, with a number of us having varying levels of life-impacting care needs. It's worth mentioning that not every person in a household needs to be regulated for it to have a positive impact, and that we all move in and out of our 'window of tolerance' daily, just relatively and at different speeds. (The window of tolerance was originally described by Dr. Dan Siegal as the optimal zone of arousal in which a person would be able to function and deal with day-to-day stress most effectively — *mind my peelings.com (2019)*.)

	Window of Tolerance Model		
	Hyperarousal	Fight and Flight	
	Dysregulated	Tired and wired	
Stress reduces the window of tolerance	Window of tolerance	Safe and social - Regulated	Self-care expands the window of tolerance
	Dysregulated	Shutting down	
	Hypoarousal	Freeze	

This is not about happy families and perfect parenting. Far from it. This is about being able to prioritise moments of regulation (in whatever safe way it can be achieved) throughout each day, as much as is possible with our unique circumstances. It doesn't need to be perfect, just valued and unapologetically practised. Eventually we may find we are able to stay in this regulated state longer, despite the external challenges. Some of us need help accessing it initially, but once we know what we're aiming for and the more regulated we can become, the more felt sense of safety we can offer our children when they are struggling.

A parent who can regularly prioritise responding to needs (including their own) — play, sensory regulation, gratitude, finding glimmers of joy in the tricky, and honouring and processing emotions healthily — is often (not all of the time) able to bring about shared benefits. And the beauty is that it can work both ways, as a regulated child can also influence the state of their parent.

So, this is about permission to acknowledge how hard it is and find ways to process that. (Process art can be great for this, as our children don't know what our 'art' represents.) It's also permission to give yourself the biggest break that many (including yourself) often aren't queueing up to give you.

How dysregulation can present

Some of us have lived in stressful or over-stimulating circumstances for so long that we're not even aware we're dysregulated, especially when we have children with additional needs and/or particularly challenging ongoing circumstances. So, to learn how to find a sense of calm and balance we may need to observe the ways in which our dysregulation can present.

This is by no means an exhaustive list, but dysregulation indicators include: a general sense of unease, breathlessness or air hunger, tense muscles, clenched jaw, racing heartbeat, tinnitus, sensory sensitivities, irritability, racing thoughts, critical thoughts, a sense of disassociation or numbness, or significantly heightened connection to emotions, anxiety, temperature dysregulation, dizziness, hypervigilance, and more. Do you relate to any? Many of us probably do. We are human, after all.

How regulation can present

Many people have not had the advantage of being able to experience a fully regulated state in their lifetime, so it's important to include what regulating looks like, too.

Yawning, sighing, relaxing muscles, sense of calm, trust and wellbeing, rest, slowing of pace, joy, playfulness, awe, wonder, hopeful anticipation, appreciation of a moment, acceptance, self-compassion, and an ability to transition relatively quickly between states of fight, flight, and freeze (NB: these are healthy protective responses we all experience and need; we're just not meant to stay stuck in them).

Again, we don't need to be regulated all of the time or even fully. We just need to be able to access it the best we can in a healthy way. In this calmer state we can recover from or better manage a wide variety of symptoms and also develop, learn, and create new possibilities.

Core needs

When we enter the world as babies, other than milk, clothes, and nappies, we need safety, love, and connection. We are designed to regulate to our caregivers through touch and playful, loving connection, but this can be experienced differently from person to person, especially if we or our children are experiencing difficulties with providing or receiving those things. If we are struggling in this way, it's usually a sign that we may benefit from some specialised support.

It can be particularly helpful to remember these core needs when we or a family member are struggling on any level. Think about a time you felt completely overwhelmed. What did you need? A solution, or to be accepted, loved, and supported in a way you could uniquely respond to? Solutions are best explored at a time when we are calm.

What activities do you and/or your children do that create a sense of safety and connection? It could be anything from playing with water and ripping paper, to having a drink in the sunshine (or a dimly lit room), being creative, active, and so much more. When life has become too much for us, these things become incredibly important in sending our bodies cues of calm and safety and are more valuable than we can realise. And if we are poorly ourselves, supporting our children to regulate in a safe way can give us space to pace ourselves better.

Co-regulating through rapport

If we can understand how we regulate ourselves, we can also influence and guide our children. In short, when we relax and respond from a place of calm, trust, and self-compassion, our children can and will calibrate (to varying degrees and depending on their own skills and needs). For children with significant challenges and dysregulation, this becomes even more necessary, yet we're often not equipped to know how to support their unique needs, and it's a whole new education for us.

Rapport is something that the majority take for granted. Many go through life with little to no awareness of its existence yet experience the benefits of unconsciously tuning into and calibrating with those around them. What exactly is rapport? It can look like two people chatting animatedly and waving their hands in the air with similar gestures, unconsciously mimicking someone's tone of voice, sitting in comfortable silence, matching someone's speed of walking, talking, or even breathing, or even children playing alongside each other, not necessarily 'with' each other. Rapport, put simply, is moments of harmonious togetherness.

However, 'typical' rapport doesn't come naturally to all of us. For some children and adults, especially those with a lowered or heightened sensitivity to their environment and/or communication differences, rapport can be difficult to achieve. Actually, we are all capable of rapport, but in some cases it's only achieved when we're with people who can relate to our experience in some way or those who find a way to meet us where we are.

If we have a child who has an intense interest and is struggling to focus on anything else, that's where we need to start in order to connect and build rapport. It's through their experience of acceptance, safety, and connection that they might (when they are ready) start to build on the skills needed to expand their experience.

Hidden barriers

In reality, we don't live in a society that supports nervous system regulation. We're in a hustle culture of productivity, chronically stressed, isolated (often more so if we have children with additional needs), and attempting to live up to expectations that our bodies aren't always in a position to meet or in fact designed to.

And a denial of basic needs is glamourised everywhere we turn. We applaud productivity over rest and will do anything to keep going to prove our worth. Our value can often be unconsciously rooted in productivity, and this is constantly confirmed by the world around us. So, when we find ourselves in the unfortunate position of our bodies saying 'no thank you very much, I'm not designed to do this' on a cellular level, it can feel like we've failed.

Often the additional pressure that comes from within is a complex mix of emotions, beliefs, expectations, and values that we may have outgrown due to our circumstances. So, it can be helpful to ask ourselves, what do I believe in this situation? What is needed right now? What might get us close to that? Do we just need to survive this moment? This will pass eventually, and sometimes that has to be enough.

The challenge

As parents, our sole focus is usually on helping our children and finding answers, especially if they are struggling. We may not even recognise when we ourselves become dysregulated. It's incredibly irritating to be told that you can't pour from an empty cup or that you need to look after yourself in this scenario, especially when we are doing everything in our power just to hold things together with minimal or non-existent outside support. Hence the caveat earlier. There are periods of time where, if possible, we just have to push through in the best way we can. But many out there have found out the hard way that there is a limit to how long the body will continue to function like this.

It can feel counterintuitive to seek help for ourselves when we are just holding everything together. We may not know what help we need, and what's offered can sometimes just add pressure rather than reduce it. However, if we can learn how to reduce the impact stress is having on us, or at least find regular opportunities to be in our 'window of tolerance', our children can experience the benefits and learn the value (and sometimes a few tools that will in turn help them).

How do I know this? Through all our trials as a family dealing with illness, disability, and the systemic challenges that come with that, I have some really precious memories. And guess what? They all involve some level of co-regulation. Even during our crisis years. Swinging on a basket swing with a child, momentarily calmed, lying on top of me, time seemingly standing still for a moment. Playing music and blowing bubbles, sitting in a ball pit experiencing deep pressure together, doing process art for fun, but also to change our focus and do something accessible for all of us together.

I recently spoke to someone I had worked with during my therapeutic coaching training. She shared that one of the strategies she had learnt during our sessions was not only effective and something she was still using to this day, but that one of her children had observed her using it and reminded her about it in a stressful moment. So, looking after ourselves in this way will not only help in the moment but also model the need for boundaries and self-care to be able to give the best of ourselves as much as is possible — something our children need to be able to do, too.

How do we do this?

There are different levels of nervous system dysregulation. If you just need to keep going and can do so, then it's about taking pauses, refocusing to a calmer state, and carrying on. If, however, you are struggling to function and are reaching or have reached burnout, you might need some supportive help to gain deeper insight. We can't always change our circumstances but sometimes we can change how we respond to them in a way that supports us rather than continues to deplete us. For those who are neurodivergent (differing in mental or neurological function from what is considered 'typical'), there are increasing numbers of counsellors and coaches, including myself, who are neurodivergent-affirming. If CBT or regular counselling hasn't helped, it's worth looking for someone offering a trauma-informed and client-led approach.

In-the-moment strategies

- Pausing and taking a breath

- Breathing in and exhaling for longer (outbreath activates the parasympathetic — safe and social system)

- Tapping just below your collarbone

- Looking into the distance and moving your gaze from side to side

- Prayer

- Reassuring self-talk

Medium strategies

- Appropriate exercise or movement

- Sensory play

- Mindful walks, noticing what you see, hear, smell, feel. Taking photos can be helpful for keeping focus.

- Process art — art with no aim, just mark-making to music or emotions

- Journaling — no-one has to read it, but it can be a great way of expressing things you don't feel able to elsewhere. You can even burn it afterwards.

- Singing or humming

- Sitting with a drink

- Doing something you enjoy

Longer strategies

- Learn about your emotions and what they are signalling to you

- Explore your beliefs and values — especially noticing if you feel pulled in different directions at times

- Process the things that are distressing you, either with a friend or consider a counsellor or therapeutic coach

Dedication

Thank you to my family. There aren't adequate words. I love you and thank you for everything. Society may not be set up with families like ours in mind, but we don't need to be defeated.

Biography

Sarah, a former music teacher, is a faith-filled wife and mum of two children, both neurodivergent. One is in mainstream education, another who has higher support needs attends a broad-spectrum special school. Sarah has also dealt with various chronic conditions over her lifetime.

Her continuing recovery over the last four years from moderate/severe long Covid has led to her retraining as a therapeutic coach, specialising in nervous system retraining. She has a deeper understanding of the challenges that her youngest faces and is grateful for the similarities her experience has allowed her to observe when the nervous system is stuck in a dysregulated state.

Parent caring when dealing with chronic illness is extremely challenging. Yet we do it, often with little support or true understanding of ourselves or our loved ones.

Creativity is a much-valued resource, and Sarah often spends time in nature with her camera. She also uses art, humour, music, and imagination to navigate the daily obstacle course that is being a parent carer.

If you would like support with the challenges that you are facing and to find a way to navigate them from a place of acceptance, understanding, and hope, please do reach out.

You can connect with Sarah here:

https://linktr.ee/SarahBurnettCoaching

Self-Care when Caring for Mental Health
By Duncan Casburn

'It's not selfish to be self-caring' — *Duncan Casburn*

I can remember an old ad from TV. In it there was a young child having a meltdown in a supermarket, with the dad looking on in embarrassment and shame. It turned out to be an ad for condoms. I must confess, early on in parenthood, I felt this way myself on some occasions.

To explain, my daughter is autistic with a PDA profile. PDA, or Pathological Demand Avoidance, is a profile on the autism spectrum. A very basic explanation of PDA is as follows:

Pathological Demand Avoidance is a condition associated with Autism Spectrum Disorder (ASD). It is a rare behavioural phenotype of ASD that is characterised by an overwhelming or obsessional need to resist or avoid demands, which can often lead to sensory overwhelm causing meltdowns and violent outbursts. (Source: The ACT Group)

The important thing to note here is that my daughter can't help this. It's not a conscious decision to 'be naughty', but a subconscious need for control in order to subdue her anxiety.

My daughter is my world. She's my firstborn, she's caring, funny, intelligent, and amazing. The PDA is very challenging, but her autism and PDA are both intrinsic parts of who she is, and I wouldn't change her.

She's now fourteen, and as we all know, that means the dreaded adolescent years are in full swing. As you can probably imagine, PDA and pubescent hormones don't mix well; in fact, they're the recipe for disaster!

Over the last twelve months in particular, I have seen my daughter's mental health plummet. We've been through issues with her mental health over the years, and we've always got through it. But seeing our beautiful kids suffer is too much to bear sometimes. It hurts me to see how much she's hurting and feeling so unable to help her.

And that's where I want to focus — on how I, as a dad, feel in all this. How do I help her? How do I avoid burnout? How do I manage my mental health in all this?

This may seem a little selfish, but I honestly believe that if we want to be the best for our kids, we have to exercise self-care. It's not selfish to be self-caring.

As parents and carers, it's natural to put ourselves last on the list of priorities... and rightly so. As a dad and husband, I see my role as ensuring my family have all their needs met. I don't mean that in a sexist way; I am an equal with my wife! What I mean is that, as a wise man once told me, 'Our role as parents and husbands isn't exercising control, rather what am I going to sacrifice for them today?'

To add a complexity to this, my wife is not well, with both physical and mental disabilities. This means that if I were to collapse in despair or fail to look after myself physically and mentally — if I were unable to be the husband and father I have to be — my family would really suffer.

As such, especially in times like those we're currently dealing with, taking time to manage my own wellbeing is not selfish, it's essential!

What follows are some of the lessons I've learnt, some of the mistakes I've made, and some of the successes we've achieved.

Owning my mistakes, whilst showing myself compassion

If I were to list all my mistakes, a chapter in a book wouldn't be nearly enough. In fact, it would look more like the old leather-bound Encyclopaedia Britannica sets!

We all make mistakes, but the difference is how we use them. They can be sources of guilt, shame, self-pity, or even anger. Or they can be lessons learned, ways to move forward and be better in the future.

Guilt, in particular, is a massive issue. Speaking for myself, I think it may be the biggest source of self-destructive behaviours I have. I'm my own worst critic, and many times this has led me to suffering crippling self-doubt and made situations far worse than they could have been.

For example, on many occasions I've lost my temper when my daughter has been in meltdown. She has this amazing ability to focus on my biggest insecurities and drive the proverbial dagger into these perceived weaknesses when she's in that meltdown mode. And my response, on occasion, has been to lose my temper and shout back at her. This is immediately followed (quite rightly) by crushing guilt.

That guilt is so important, as it lets me know I've done wrong. But it would continue to eat me up all day. My daughter would pick up on this and blame herself, thinking I was still angry at her, and this would feed back into her anxiety, causing more meltdowns. The very definition of a vicious cycle.

I had to learn to forgive myself. I had to acknowledge my wrong but then draw a line under it and move on... not giving myself a 'free pass' but rather investing in trying to make sure my daughter wasn't feeding off my guilt.

Add to this, dwelling on guilt is not good for mental health. Guilt has a sneaky way of constantly popping into our heads, reminding us that we're 'not worthy' because we did this or that. It can become all-consuming — and that helps nobody.

Self-compassion is essential to our being able to learn from our mistakes, but we can't let them be a source of constant negativity.

Emotion windows

Last night my daughter was in tears. She told me how low she was feeling, how lonely she is, and how she just wishes she was 'like other girls'. I had to hold it together and reassure her that she will be okay. I hugged her and soothed her, but inside my heart was breaking.

As a teen, I went through similar experiences myself. The feelings of loneliness and not fitting in are issues many of us face at some point in our lives. Hearing my daughter share her feelings brought those painful memories right back. But it was worse because they were happening to her.

There have been other times that I've been overcome with anger. As I said before, my daughter has a talent for targeting my most vulnerable insecurities. There are times when she says things so cutting and hurtful that I flare up inside, feeling rage as she attacks me.

I have to suppress these emotions, as to show them at the time would cause more issues. But I *do* have the right to feel these things, and repressing them could easily lead to problems. But how do I allow these feelings to come out without them causing bigger issues at the time?

The answer is to allow myself *Emotion Windows*. When the time is right, when things have calmed down and I can remove myself briefly, I allow these emotions to be expressed. I allow myself a window of time to be able to feel my feelings. Sometimes I may be alone, and suddenly the emotions hit me from nowhere. In the past these emotions have lasted all day, or longer.

We have the right to feel what we feel, be it despair, anger, worry, whatever. And when these emotions surface, they need to be acknowledged. My problem in the past was that they'd consume me and overtake me. Allowing myself to have a window of time to feel what I need to feel, but saying to myself that I have ten minutes, twenty minutes, half an hour even, allows me to deal with my emotional needs without them becoming overwhelming.

It's another example of self-compassion; understanding that we need to acknowledge our feelings without letting them fester for too long.

Talk; for the love of God, talk!

When this latest episode of my daughter's mental health issues came to the surface, I did the worst thing I could. I sort of shut myself away, and I didn't talk to anyone about it.

The strange thing is that I constantly advise people to make sure they're talking to others, to make sure they have that moral support... so why was I not heeding my own advice?

The answer came, ironically, from talking to a friend. Noticing that I'd been quiet, she reached out to me and wanted to make sure I was ok. Thank goodness she did!

I was quite happy to talk about things once prompted, so why was I not openly discussing things with people whom I know care about me?

I realised that it wasn't because I didn't want to, and it wasn't that I feared judgement or making myself vulnerable. It was actually that I didn't want to burden others with my problems.

Peel back the layers of any person's life and you'll find that they have difficulties going on. Show me someone who doesn't, and I'll show you a liar. And this knowledge was what was holding me back. Why would I burden someone else with my own challenges when they already had theirs to deal with?

I think that this is something a lot of men feel. We often get accused of being too shut off or guarding our emotions too closely. For me, this isn't the case. It's not that I don't want to share myself; it's that I don't want to add more problems to someone else's life.

As I discussed this with my friend, she understood and told me a story that totally changed my perspective. She (we'll call her Jane) told me about one of her closest friends who was battling cancer.

Jane was facing a health scare of her own and wanted to talk to her bestie about it, but she felt — like I do — that her challenges were far less important, and didn't want to burden her friend with things. Eventually this friend noticed Jane was holding back and asked her directly what was wrong. Jane opened up and told her, explaining that, with all the other woman was going through, she didn't want her worrying about anything else.

Jane's friend gave the best response ever. 'Of course I want to know. I may be ill, but I'm still here, and helping you would give me reason to keep going. Even just listening to you gives me a purpose. And you've been such a support to me, I want to be the same for you!'

In the same way, *my* friends want to help and support me. I have a couple of close friends I know I can talk to. There's not much anyone can do practically in our current situation, but knowing that I can pick up the phone to them, or go grab a coffee, is so amazing. Sometimes we don't even talk about what's going on. A couple of weeks ago I went to my neighbour's house, and we just had a few drinks and listened to music. It was brilliant and completely lifted my mood.

So, talk. Find that person who you can trust and be open with. Trust me, they *want* to help!

An extra point to add here. I came to this understanding about myself because a friend *reached out to me*. If you suspect that someone you know is going through hard times, reach out to them. It can be this simple act that makes a huge difference in their lives. It might even save a life!

Hold onto hope

With everything my family is facing at the moment, it's far too easy to lose hope. We've all heard the old saying: 'The light at the end of the tunnel is an oncoming train.' Man, it definitely feels that way at times. Every time I think we've overcome an issue, another one pops up to replace it. If feels like a celestial game of Whack-a-mole!

So, I have to remind myself that this current situation isn't forever. We've gone through difficulties before, and we will get through this, too. Even though things suck now, they *will* get better again.

And I mean this in both the long and short term.

Long term, things will improve. Life is a rollercoaster not a train ride. We will always have our ups and downs, and that is how it is for us all.

But I need to remember this in the short term as well. When my daughter has a meltdown, or is in tears with depression, this too is temporary. This moment will pass.

For me, this means being able to draw a line under it and move on. In times past, I used to find a morning meltdown would ruin my whole day, especially if my daughter had hit me or smashed something valuable.

What I realise now is that this was because I'd carry the resentment which I felt with me. I didn't realise it at the time, but I would become moody and grumpy, and this would show in my face and body language, even in my tone of voice.

I've had to learn to draw a line after each moment. I can allow myself to have an emotion window, but I have to move on. Otherwise, my daughter picks up on my emotions and it feeds her anxiety, leading to more meltdowns (in much the same way as I said about guilt above).

To sum up

This will shock many, but I'm not perfect! None of us are. In an age of social media, where everyone only shows a filtered view of their perfect lives, it can feel like we're alone. But I promise you, you're not.

YOU MATTER! You are so important in your kids' lives, in your family's lives, and in the lives of others. As I said before, it's not selfish to be self-caring. Make that your mantra as you move forward. Be compassionate to yourself. Let go of past mistakes. Allow yourself to feel and talk things through with someone you trust. This IS only temporary!

When your kids suffer mental health issues, they need you more than ever. To be the best for them, make sure you're at your best for you, too.

Dedication:

For Sienna: you will light up this world!

Biography:

Duncan Casburn is a devoted father of a wonderful daughter with Autism and PDA (Pathological Demand Avoidance), embracing the highs and lows of neurodiverse parenting. He has a YouTube channel — PDA DAD UK — reflecting his life, a fusion of personal narratives, shared experiences, and informative content.

PDA Dad UK is a dedicated space for understanding Autism, Pathological Demand Avoidance, and the broader spectrum of neurodiversities, and the channel unravels not just the 'what' but the 'who' behind these conditions. While the terms Autism and PDA are commonly recognised, true understanding is often lacking, and that's where the channel comes in. Every video is a heart-to-heart conversation, a professional insight, or a beacon of enlightenment on the nuances of neurodiversity.

Beyond just sharing, Duncan holds roles that connect him deeper into this community, serving as a Carers' Ambassador for Devon

Carers, an Ambassador Volunteer for DiAS (Devon Information Advice and Support), and an Ambassador for the PDA Society.

You can connect with Duncan here:

https://linktr.ee/PDADadUK

The Power of Breath

Supporting Your Child's Physical, Mental, and Emotional Wellbeing By Fleur Conway

'Breath is the essence of life — gentle yet powerful, guiding and shaping the rhythm of our days and night.' — Fleur Conway

As parents, we all want our children to grow, learn, and thrive. But what if something as simple as how they breathe is holding them back? Breathing is automatic, but when it becomes dysfunctional — like chronic mouth breathing or shallow breathing — it can impact a child's brain development, emotions, sleep, and even school and sports performance. In this chapter, I want to share why optimal breathing is essential for your child's development and how simple changes can support their emotional resilience and ability to thrive.

The information I'm sharing with you on dysfunctional breathing may seem overwhelming at first. But if any of the signs I mention resonate with your child's breathing patterns or overall wellbeing, don't worry — there is so much you can do as a parent to better their breathing. And that's the amazing thing about breathing! Even though it's an automatic function, it's also something we can modify and improve with the right knowledge and guidance. *Small, simple changes can make a big difference!*

As you read through this, you might notice that some of these signs feel familiar to you as well. The guidance in this chapter isn't just for your child; it can be beneficial for you, too! Remember, children naturally mimic their parents and caregivers, so taking a moment to reflect and improve on your own breathing pattern will help your child improve theirs.

At the end of the chapter, I'll share simple, practical steps you can take to help improve your child's breathing as well as your own.

So, let's go ahead and talk about breathing!

Breathing isn't just about oxygen. Proper breathing plays a crucial role in all our bodily functions: efficient oxygen delivery to cells; supports a strong immune system; maintains the body's ideal pH levels; hormone balance; digestion; blood circulation; cognition; and ensures the nervous system functions smoothly. Carbon dioxide (CO_2) (produced by our metabolism) plays a key role in this process by helping oxygen release from the blood into the tissues, supporting brain function and maintaining a calm, balanced state. Breathing also influences posture, which is essential for a child's growth, development, and movement.

But many parents don't realise that their child may be struggling with a dysfunctional breathing pattern. Some signs can be obvious, like constant mouth breathing or snoring, while others are more subtle. If your child has a permanent stuffy nose, enlarged tonsils, suffers from asthma, allergies, or sore throats, it could be a sign that their breathing isn't as perfect as it should be. Other signs might include irritability, difficulty eating with their mouth closed, restless sleep, bedwetting, or even struggles with focus and concentration at school and lack of energy or hyperactivity during the day. These issues are often overlooked or seen as 'normal' childhood complaints, but they could indicate an underlying problem with how your child breathes.

We must understand that optimal breathing is key for all physiological processes, and there is continuous two-way feedback between breath, sleep, and the mind.

Our nose is for breathing and smelling and our mouth is for eating, drinking, laughing, talking, singing, and kissing. You wouldn't eat through your nose, so why breathe through your mouth? This is what I repeat and repeat to all children... and they get it!

Our nose is designed for breathing (it is the entrance to the respiratory system), while our mouth is not (it is the entrance to our digestive system). The nose acts as a natural air filter, warming, humidifying, and cleaning the air before it reaches the lungs. It also produces nitric oxide, which helps improve lung blood circulation, gas exchange, and supports immune function. In contrast, the mouth has no built-in filtration system, making it easier for unfiltered, dry hot or cold air to enter the lungs, which in turn can lead to infections, inflammation, bronchoconstriction, and poor oxygen delivery.

Did you know that breathing issues can begin as early as in infancy?

Even as babies, children can show early signs of dysfunctional breathing patterns. If your baby has trouble latching while breastfeeding, frequently gasps for air, has frequent colic, or sleeps with their mouth open, these could be early indicators of an airway or breathing issue. Some babies may develop a habit of snoring or noisy breathing while they sleep. Many of these early signs are connected to bad tongue position, nasal congestion, or a restricted airway. Babies are natural nasal breathers, but when something interferes with this, it will set the stage for future challenges.

Dysfunctional breathing patterns can also develop later — after a bad cold or flu, a traumatic experience, or due to an underlying anatomical issue. The problem is that once the original cause has been resolved — for example, a bad cold — the new dysfunctional breathing habit often remains uncorrected and becomes ingrained, continuing to affect the child's health and development.

But what happens as these children grow into teenagers and young adults?

Dysfunctional breathing doesn't just disappear — it continues to shape their health, emotional wellbeing, and ability to cope with stress and everyday life. Teens dealing with poor breathing patterns may experience more anxiety, difficulty concentrating, hyperactivity, sleep disturbances, and even lower self-confidence. A racing mind, forgetfulness, mood swings, and chronic fatigue or apathy are often linked to poor oxygenation and nervous system dysregulation caused by inefficient breathing. Over time, this will affect their academic performance, social interactions, and even their ability to enjoy sports or other physical activities.

Addressing these concerns early and working with a specialist can help lay the foundation for healthy breathing patterns as your child grows.

There are many cognitive therapies and meditations available to help with a racing mind and anxiety, but here's the key: if the foundation — every day, every night habitual breathing — isn't addressed first, the underlying issue will persist. Dysfunctional breathing patterns don't just happen during moments of stress; they are present 24/7, shaping a person's entire experience of life. This is exactly what I do in my every day —help address and correct habitual dysfunctional breathing patterns, so that children, teens, and adults can breathe better, feel better, and truly thrive.

How breathing shapes thinking and emotions

Breathing is deeply connected to how the brain functions. Every breath we take influences brain activity, alertness, and emotional regulation. The brain and breath are constantly communicating — when we breathe well, we think better, feel calmer, and perform at our best.

Poor breathing, on the other hand, can keep the brain in a hyped-up 'mode', making the brain feel like it's in a constant state of stress. Shallow or rapid breathing tells the body that something is wrong, triggering the nervous system into a state of heightened alertness. This can make it harder for children to concentrate, control impulses, and regulate their emotions.

When breathing is slow, deep, and nasal, the brain receives the right amount of oxygen and carbon dioxide balance, allowing children to stay focused, concentrate, remember things, stay calm and in control of situations.

Have you ever noticed how your child's breathing changes when they're upset or anxious? One of the most fascinating connections in the body is between breathing and the amygdala — the part of the brain responsible for processing emotions, especially fear and anxiety. When breathing is fast and shallow, the amygdala interprets this as a sign of danger, triggering the fight-or-flight response. When this happens regularly, children can become more anxious, restless, and have a harder time managing their emotions. This is why children who breathe poorly may seem more anxious, irritable, or emotionally reactive.

On the other hand, slow, controlled nasal breathing sends a signal to the amygdala that everything is safe. This helps children feel more grounded, relaxed, and emotionally balanced. Many relaxation techniques — including mindfulness and meditation — are based on breathing exercises because of their ability to calm the mind, the amygdala, and lower stress hormones. But remember, while these techniques can be incredibly powerful, their benefits won't be long-lasting if the underlying dysfunctional breathing pattern isn't addressed. *It's like putting a bandage on a broken bone — helpful in the moment, but not a true fix.* That's why building a strong foundation of optimal breathing is key. It allows these relaxation techniques to work more effectively and create lasting change.

Breath and sleep: The essential connection

We all know how much kids need good sleep to grow, learn, and be their best selves. But what if their breathing is preventing them from getting the deep, restorative rest they need? If your child snores, breathes through their mouth at night, or constantly tosses and turns, dysfunctional breathing could be the hidden culprit.

If your child isn't sleeping well, their breathing may be playing a bigger role than you realise. Sleep is when the brain processes information, strengthens memory, detoxifies, and restores energy levels. If a child's breathing is disrupted — whether due to mouth breathing, snoring, an obstructed airway, or sleep apnoea — it can lead to restless nights and poor-quality sleep.

When children breathe through their mouths at night, they often wake up feeling tired, even after a full night's sleep. This happens because mouth breathing reduces oxygen absorption and can cause frequent subtle awakenings. A lack of deep sleep affects emotional stability, energy levels, and even immune function. Over time, poor sleep due to dysfunctional breathing can contribute to or be the underlying cause of poor concentration at school, learning difficulties, low energy, emotional struggles, behavioural issues, and increased stress levels.

How breathing affects behaviour and social interaction

Does your child seem on edge or struggle with social interactions? Dysfunctional breathing can keep them in a constant state of alertness, making it difficult to relax and engage with others. It can also contribute to mood swings, making small frustrations feel like big emotional outbursts.

When a child is stuck in a pattern of shallow or mouth breathing, their autonomic nervous system remains in a heightened state. This can make them more reactive to stress, more easily overwhelmed by changes in their environment, and less able to cope with everyday challenges. Over time, this heightened stress response can impact their ability to interact. They may avoid social situations because they feel anxious or too exhausted to participate, or they may struggle with emotional regulation, which can make interactions with peers more difficult.

Breathing also plays a role in self-esteem. When children feel constantly tired, on edge, or unable to concentrate, they may start to doubt themselves. They might struggle in school, find it hard to keep up with sports or activities, or feel different from their peers. Over time, this can erode their confidence and make them hesitant to try new things.

Mouth breathing and facial development

You may not have realised it, but how your child breathes influences the development of their face, teeth, and jaw! Long-term mouth breathing can lead to noticeable changes in facial structure and dental health.

The tongue plays a crucial role in proper jaw and facial development. It should naturally rest on the roof of the mouth, helping to guide the upper jaw into the right shape. But when a child mouth breathes, the mouth opens and their tongue sits lower, which can lead to long-term structural changes and even restriction and narrowing of the upper airway.

If your child breathes through their mouth regularly, you might see:

- Overcrowded teeth or a high-arched palate

- A longer, narrower face and jaw development

- More cavities due to a dry mouth

- Speech difficulties

Dysfunctional breathing and PMS

Dysfunctional breathing can also have an impact on teenage girls' menstrual cycles and PMS symptoms. The way we breathe affects our body's oxygen and carbon dioxide balance, which in turn influences hormone regulation and pain perception. When breathing is shallow or rapid, it can increase cortisol, which as we know is the 'stress' hormone.

Teenagers who breathe improperly may experience more severe premenstrual symptoms, including mood swings, fatigue, bloating, and cramps. Shallow breathing keeps the body in a low-grade stress state, which can make PMS symptoms feel more intense and prolonged. Additionally, poor breathing patterns can contribute to poor sleep quality, which further exacerbates hormonal fluctuations and discomfort during the menstrual cycle.

Breaking the habit of dysfunctional breathing

Breathing is something we do automatically, but the way we breathe often becomes a learned habit. Just like a child can develop the habit of slouching or biting their nails, they may also develop a habit of mouth breathing, breathing more rapidly, or taking shallow breaths. Over time, their body can adapt to this inefficient breathing pattern, even though it is not the most optimal way to breathe.

Just like any habit, improving breathing takes patience and practice, and the key is to make small, consistent changes. The more you support and gently remind your child to breathe properly, the easier it will become for them. Over time, this important change will improve their sleep, focus, and overall wellbeing — setting them up for a lifetime of healthy breathing.

Remember, breath is a gift — one that has the power to shape your child's future.

Let's make sure they are using it to their greatest advantage.

As a parent, you have the power to make small but impactful changes that support your child's breathing and wellbeing. By focusing on your child's breathing, you are giving them a lifelong tool for managing stress, improving focus, and maintaining emotional balance. Breathing well is not just about physical health — it's about equipping our children with the ability to navigate life's challenges with confidence and ease.

Here are a few simple steps you can take:

1. Observe your child's breathing, tongue position, and sleep pattern. This is the first step to determine if it's necessary to seek professional advice.

2. Encourage nasal breathing, which helps protect overall health, supports proper development, and ensures the body functions at its best. Remind your child to breathe through their nose instead of their mouth. At home, simple techniques like saline rinses, gentle nose-clearing exercises, and encouraging hydration, can help make nasal breathing easier. If they struggle, this may be a sign of an airway issue that should be assessed by a specialist.

3. Practise breathing exercises together. Simple breathing techniques, such as humming (with the mouth closed) for 5 minutes, 2-3 times a day, and walking whilst breathing through nose (*so no talking!*) can help your child feel calmer and more focused. More specific exercises like breath-holds should ideally be taught initially by a certified breathing instructor for proper execution.

4. Limit screen time before bed. Excessive screen time can contribute to poor sleep and increased stress and neural hyperactivity.

5. Create a relaxing bedtime environment. Make sure their bedroom is tidy, aired, and is cool. This will promote better sleep.

6. Monitor their posture. Slouching or forward head posture can restrict proper breathing, movement, and self-esteem. Looking down at mobile phones will also influence this, so gentle reminders to sit up straight, stand tall, and look forward, will help healthy posture and breathing mechanics.

7. Teaching proper tongue posture is crucial for optimal nose

and mouth development. Practising simple tongue exercises, like clicking the tongue on the roof of the mouth 30-50 times twice a day can help keep the tongue in its natural resting position. If your child has difficulty placing their tongue on the roof of the mouth (hard palate) then it would be advisable to check for tongue tie.

By making small adjustments now, you're giving your child the foundation for better breathing, better sleep, and a healthier, happier future!

Dedication:

To all children —
Those who are, those who were, and those yet to be.

Biography:

Fleur Conway is a Certified Master Instructor in the Buteyko Method, trained by the world's leading school in this transformative breathing approach. She specialises in respiratory re-education in children and adults for conditions such as asthma, allergies, mouth breathing, chronic rhinitis, sleep-disordered breathing, menopause symptoms, ADHD, and more. As an Advanced Oxygen Advantage Instructor, she focuses on sports performance and Intermittent Hypoxic Training. Fleur is also a Low Pressure Fitness Trainer, Life & Menopause Coach, and Bach Flower Therapist.

Passionate about holistic wellbeing, she integrates her expertise to help individuals achieve balance in breath, mind, and body. She collaborates with orthodontists, myofunctional therapists, and educational institutions, to promote healthy breathing habits in the younger generation. Fleur actively participates in international summits, instructor training, podcasts, and children's literature projects. Offering sessions in Spanish and English, she reaches diverse communities through individual coaching, workshops, and training programmes. She continues expanding her expertise in myofunctional therapy and female health.

You can connect with Fleur here:

https://linktr.ee/Coreprana

When School Feels Impossible

Understanding Autistic Burnout, Emotionally-Based School Avoidance, and the Restorative Magic of Hypno-Stories By Amy Dalwood-Fairbanks

'Stories are medicine... They have such power; they do not require that we do, be, act, anything — we need only listen.' — Clarissa Pinkola Estés, Women Who Run with the Wolves

Sammy's Story

It seemed like a typical Thursday afternoon as Dawn waited outside her ten-year-old son's classroom at home time. Usually, Sammy would bound out of school with his friends, a big smile on his face. But today was different. He emerged slowly, shoulders slumped, head down, barely acknowledging his teacher's praise for being invited to compete in the County Cross Country Championships.

Sammy was normally full of chatter, spilling out every detail of his day the moment he saw his mum. But today, he was silent. Dawn knew school could be overwhelming for him — an unpredictable mix of noise, bright lights, conflicting smells, the discomfort of his uniform, unspoken social rules, and relentless expectations. Yet he enjoyed being with his friends and had learned to mask — copying others, suppressing his need to move or escape, and enduring the discomfort until he made it home. Most days, that pent-up tension would explode the moment he walked through the door. But today was different.

When they got home, Dawn went to prepare a snack while Sammy headed upstairs to change into comfy clothes. After a while, noticing he hadn't come back down, she went to check on him. There he was, half-changed out of his uniform, fast asleep on his bed, completely drained.

The following morning, Dawn knocked on Sammy's door to wake him up to get ready for school. 'Come on, Sammy, time for school.' Silence. She opened the door to find him huddled under the duvet, eyes squeezed shut. 'I can't,' he whispered, his body rigid, his face pale.

There was no way Dawn was going to get Sammy into school today… or any day for the next few weeks, months, or possibly years.

For children like Sammy, traditional approaches and interventions to get them back into the classroom often fail. But there is a gentler way. This chapter explores how hypno-stories can provide comfort, regulation, and connection, helping children feel safe, seen, and supported.

Emotionally-Based School Avoidance

'But they're fine once they're in school!' say schoolteachers and staff all over the UK. Yet parents like Dawn are only too aware of how much effort it takes for their neurodivergent child to endure six hours in an environment which causes them so much discomfort, anxiety, and fear. It's no wonder that the morning battle of getting children into school is so common, and that so many children are unable to attend school. And no wonder emotional outbursts or meltdowns occur as soon as they get home — the only place the child feels safe. It's not defiance. It's survival.

This common behavioural response in neurodivergent children as soon as they get home is known as *After-School Restraint Collapse*, or colloquially known as 'the Coke Bottle Effect'. Think of your child's emotional regulation and wellbeing as a Coke bottle; the liquid inside symbolising their ability to hold in emotions, manage stress, and maintain self-control. Throughout the school day, their 'bottle' gets shaken by small stressors like sensory overload (buzzing lights, loud chatter) and constant rule-following (sitting still, waiting in line). Bigger shakes, like struggling with tricky work or feeling left out at playtime, add even more pressure. By home time, the bottle is so shaken that their capacity to keep everything contained is at its limit, leading to an emotional release — whether through a meltdown, shutdown, or irritability — once they reach the safety of home.

It is important that the child is allowed space to 'decompress' after school and safely let out the pressure and stress they are feeling. And once parents understand and recognise this process is not bad behaviour but essential recovery, strategies can be put in place to ensure better recovery before the next school day.

This emotional container that children have is sometimes referred to as a 'Stress Bucket', a 'Window of Tolerance', or an adapted version of 'Spoon Theory'. But when talking about After-School Restraint Collapse, I like to think of it as a battery. This analogy is easy for children to understand too, as they regularly have to think about the battery life on their phones, tablets, and other tech equipment. The ideal scenario is that the child recharges their battery every day after school and by getting a decent night's sleep. Recognising when a child's battery is low and allowing them to recharge is key to helping them manage life's challenges, while protecting their emotional health. There are many ways parents and children can work together to find ways to recharge.

Fig. 1 [Source: Itsahappyworld]

To help a child recharge their battery after school, it's important to start with low-demand activities and a predictable routine. For example, Sammy knew to go straight upstairs to change into his comfy clothes before coming down for a snack, giving him a moment to decompress. Sensory regulation can also be key — some children benefit from dim lighting, weighted blankets, or noise-cancelling headphones to soothe their overwhelmed senses. Movement helps release built-up tension, whether it's running, bouncing on a trampoline, or stretching. Others may prefer stimming, such as fidgeting with a sensory toy or listening to rhythmic music. Screen time, often criticised, can actually provide a much-needed dopamine hit, allowing a child to relax and self-regulate. Engaging in a special interest, like Sammy going for a run with his dog after school, can also be incredibly restorative, giving them a sense of joy and control. By allowing space for these recharging activities, parents can help their child recover from the day and prevent burnout.

However, problems can arise when a child cannot fully recharge their battery, often due to prolonged emotional strain, suppressed emotions, and anticipation anxiety. These ongoing stressors create a constant undercurrent of anxiety, steadily depleting their energy. Anticipation anxiety is particularly challenging, because it can be difficult for parents to recognise and hard for children to articulate. It stems from worries about future or uncertain events, like Sammy's anxiety over the County Cross Country Championships — the unknown venue, unfamiliar competitors, pressure to perform well, and endless 'what ifs' weighing heavily on his mind. Even though nothing stressful had happened yet, the worry alone drained his energy.

Autistic Burnout

If a child's battery isn't recharged daily, it runs flat. Over time, this leads to *burnout*, where recovery takes far longer, affecting mood, motivation, and overall wellbeing. Wikipedia provides a clear and well-defined explanation of autistic burnout:

'Autistic burnout is a prolonged state of intense fatigue, decreased executive functioning or life skills, and increased sensory processing sensitivity experienced by autistic people. Autistic burnout is thought to be caused by stress arising from masking or living in a neurotypical environment that is not autism-friendly (does not accommodate autistic people's needs).'

If a child's battery is already drained, they lack the capacity to handle everyday stressors at school. Even the smallest challenge can push them into burnout, while underlying anxieties may become so overwhelming that they struggle to get out of bed and face the day. Anticipation anxiety can lead to burnout even during school holidays. The stress of moving into the next school year — facing a new teacher, a different classroom, and unfamiliar routines — can drain a child's battery before the term even begins. Transitioning to a new school, especially from primary to secondary/high school, brings an overwhelming amount of change. While this is challenging for any child, it can be particularly exhausting for a neurodivergent child who already struggles with change and transitions. This is why after holidays many neurodivergent children only last a few weeks at school, and sometimes only a few days, before reaching the point of complete burnout.

Although not officially classified as a medical condition, autistic burnout is a very real and debilitating state of physical and mental exhaustion. It occurs when the nervous system becomes completely overwhelmed, leading to a shutdown that forces the body into survival mode — fight, flight, freeze, or fawn. In this state, a child may regress to behaviours that provide a sense of safety and security, becoming more dependent on their parents and struggling with even basic self-care. Unlike typical exhaustion, burnout can strip away the ability to engage in once-enjoyable special interests, leaving the child disengaged and withdrawn. Viewed through the lens of Maslow's Hierarchy of Needs, a child in burnout operates only from the bottom two levels — physiological survival, and the need for safety. Higher-level needs, such as social communication, self-esteem, and self-fulfilment, become completely out of reach. In many ways, the child's needs resemble those of a baby, requiring comfort, predictable routines, and an environment free from demands, until their nervous system has recovered enough to function again.

Fig. 2 Maslow's Hierarchy of Needs

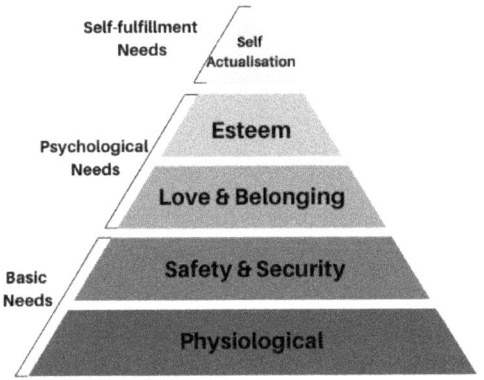

Why School Feels Impossible

If we look at Maslow's Hierarchy of Needs from the aspect of learning, we can see that a child in burnout, who is only operating from the bottom two levels, cannot in any way engage in learning and growth.

Fig. 3 Hierarchy of Needs for Learning (adapted from Platypus Training)

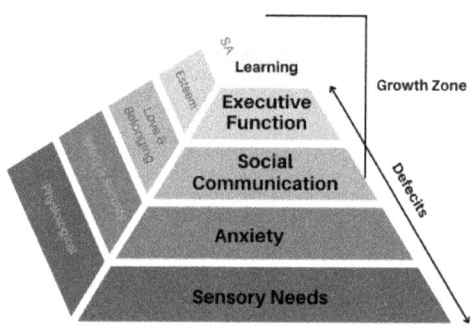

The biggest barrier for children in burnout is the inaccessibility of executive function skills. Executive function skills are the mental processes that enable individuals to plan, focus attention, remember instructions, and juggle multiple tasks successfully. These skills act as the brain's management system, helping to regulate behaviour, emotions, and cognitive tasks.

In a school setting, strong executive function skills are essential for success. Key skills include:

- **Working Memory** — Holding and using information in the mind, such as remembering instructions or recalling facts during a test.

- **Cognitive Flexibility** — Adapting to changes, problem-solving, and thinking about things in different ways, like switching between subjects or adjusting to new classroom routines.

- **Inhibitory Control** — Managing impulses and self-regulation, such as waiting for a turn to speak or resisting distractions.

- **Planning and Organisation** — Breaking tasks into steps, managing time, and keeping track of homework, books, and materials.

- **Task Initiation** — Starting work without procrastination, such as beginning an assignment without excessive prompting.

- **Emotional Regulation** — Managing frustration, anxiety, or disappointment in order to stay engaged in learning.

- **Self-Monitoring** — Assessing one's own performance and making adjustments, such as checking over work before handing it in.

Recent research indicates that the prefrontal cortex — the part of the brain responsible for executive function — is underdeveloped in neurodivergent children. As a result, when a neurodivergent child experiences burnout, executive function challenges become even more pronounced, making school particularly difficult. Tasks such as completing assignments, navigating social interactions, and managing daily transitions can feel impossible. This is why children in burnout are often unable to attend school. They simply do not have the cognitive or emotional capacity to cope with its demands.

A poll I conducted in February 2025 in the Facebook group 'Not Fine in School: Family Support for School Attendance Difficulties' (70.1k members, 5 February, 2025), showed that out of 950 parents who voted, 70% attributed Autistic Burnout (including PDA and AuDHD burnout) as the reason for their child's non-attendance at school. This is an astonishingly high number, highlighting that the school environment is not tailored to meet the needs of neurodivergent pupils.

While I won't delve into this now, parents must recognise that the education system is unlikely to change anytime soon. The understanding, support, and accommodations that neurodivergent children need from schools are often lacking, and the emphasis on cognitive-based interventions (e.g. rewards, attendance charts) and high-demand interventions (e.g. talking therapies, exposure-based approaches) are not appropriate for a child in burnout. Therefore, parents must find their own ways to support their child through burnout recovery.

The Magic of Hypno-stories

Children experiencing burnout and Emotionally-Based School Avoidance need co-regulation, a sense of safety, and low-demand emotional support. Parents need to focus on meeting their child's most fundamental physiological and emotional needs, as outlined in Maslow's Hierarchy of Needs. This is where hypno-stories play a crucial role, providing comfort, reassurance, and gentle regulation in a way that feels natural and nurturing.

Hypno-stories are soothing, sensory-friendly narratives designed to engage the subconscious mind, the part of the brain responsible for emotions, habits, and deep-seated beliefs. Unlike the conscious mind, which analyses and filters information, the subconscious mind absorbs messages more readily, especially in a state of deep relaxation. When a child listens to a hypno-story, their nervous system calms, allowing them to bypass the mental barriers that might otherwise resist reassurance or positive change. In this relaxed state, the subconscious receives the story's messages without the conscious mind shutting them out, making it easier for the child to internalise feelings of safety, confidence, and resilience.

Storytelling has always been a source of comfort, taking children back to an earlier time in their lives when bedtime stories and fairy-tales provided warmth, security, and predictability. This is particularly powerful for a child in burnout, as they need to feel safe and nurtured while recovering. Hypno-stories can be fully personalised, incorporating a child's favourite toys, people, pets, and places, even their specialist interests, which they may currently struggle to engage with in real life. Since one of the rules of the mind is that the subconscious cannot distinguish between imagination and reality, hypno-stories allow the child's body and mind to react as if these positive experiences are real. This helps rebuild confidence, self-esteem, and emotional wellbeing, gently guiding the child towards recovery in a way that feels effortless and natural.

Let's go back to Sammy's story and see what happened once I had created his own personalised hypno-story. After starting to listen to his hypno-story every night, Sammy's recovery began. The story, tailored to his interests, took him on a calming journey where he was able to run freely through a forest with his pet dog, Toby, by his side. The gentle, sensory-friendly narrative helped Sammy's mind and body relax, bypassing any cognitive overwhelm. As the story unfolded, it focused on building confidence and safety, using metaphors to frame Sammy's challenges in a way that was easy for him to process.

Over the next few weeks, Sammy's behaviour changed. He began to re-engage with self-care routines and even started getting out and walking his dog again. Sammy's mother observed that he was able to express himself more openly, and his anxiety levels decreased. The hypno-story provided Sammy with the emotional support he needed, offering him a safe space to process his burnout and gently return to a place of emotional balance. Through this approach, Sammy was able to recharge his emotional battery, restoring his sense of self. After a few months, he felt able to return to school and manage everyday demands with greater ease.

I hope this chapter has been informative and helpful in showing how we need to move away from the high-pressure, attendance-focused approach and start recognising after-school meltdowns and Emotionally-Based School Avoidance for what they really are — distress signals, not defiance. Forcing a child to push through only drains them further. Recovery has to come first. Hypno-stories provide a gentle, child-led way to support emotional regulation, helping children process stress without the pressure to talk, explain, or perform. Parents often worry about school attendance, but the truth is the more we focus on meeting a child's needs — safety, connection, and regulation — the more likely they are to re-engage with school in their own time. Recovery isn't a step back; it's the first step forward.

Dedication:

This chapter is dedicated to my two incredible children, G and V. Your strength, resilience, and unwavering spirit inspire me every day. It is because of you that I embarked on this journey to support and advocate for neurodivergent children facing challenges in school. Your experiences have shaped my passion and commitment to making the world a more understanding and supportive place for families like ours.

Biography:

Amy Dalwood-Fairbanks is a paediatric clinical hypnotherapist and the founder of Magic Minds Family Hypnotherapy. With 16 years of lived experience supporting autistic family members, including her two children who have faced challenges with anxiety, burnout, and school avoidance, Amy has a deep understanding of the unique struggles neurodivergent families encounter. She specialises in supporting children with anxiety, Emotionally-Based School Avoidance, and autistic burnout, offering bespoke Magic Moment Hypno-stories, one-to-one therapy sessions, and parent support.

Amy is passionate about promoting children's mental health and believes in the power of hypnotherapy as an effective, low-demand intervention for neurodivergent children. She is dedicated to making hypnotherapy more accessible and recognised for its transformative impact. Through writing, speaking, and sharing her insights, Amy strives to educate and advocate for a more compassionate, informed approach to neurodivergent mental health, helping children and families feel empowered, understood, and supported.

You can connect with Amy here:

https://linktr.ee/MagicMindsHypnotherapy

Nature's Classroom
Nurturing Resilience, Confidence, and Creativity Outdoors By Lucy Fenwick

'The more risks you allow your children to take, the better they learn to take care of themselves.' — Roald Dahl

Growing up by the sea, I have always felt deeply connected to nature. My childhood was spent walking the rolling South Downs, where my mum would quiz me on tree species, butterflies, and any wildlife we encountered. We spent hours quietly watching and listening, fostering a deep respect for the natural world. My mum volunteered at the local RSPB reserve, and I would join her, chatting with birdwatchers, identifying birds, and helping with litter picking. Looking after the environment was simply part of life, and that love of nature never faded.

When I became a parent, I carried that passion into raising my children. I took my first child every day into the woods or along the shoreline, immersed in the sights, sounds, and textures of the outdoors. Professionally, I trained as a primary school teacher, and my career took me to Hong Kong, where I spent ten years teaching and engaging in different environmental projects across Asia. I loved my work — it allowed me to jump about, be silly, and inspire children to be adventurous, resilient, and curious. But long hours and high demands led to moments of burnout, making me reflect on how I could balance my passion for working with children while being fully present for my own.

It was when it came time to find a school for my eldest that I first heard about Forest School. The concept resonated deeply, and I knew I had to learn more. I found a local group of like-minded women who also wanted to train, an inspiring teacher, and the perfect site in the South Downs. That magical week in the woods, learning the ethos of Forest School, bushcraft, and techniques for outdoor learning, sparked something in me. I had found my passion again.

By chance, the Forest School linked to my son's primary school had to stop running due to the leader's ill health, and I was fortunate enough to step in. That's when Lucy's Forest School was born. Initially, I worked solely with the school, but I soon found the structure of trying to fit the curriculum challenging to align with true Forest School principles. To create a more authentic experience, I launched holiday day camps, welcoming children from all backgrounds. Using school holidays allowed me to follow the principles more closely, as it gave them a long time out in the woods, and I could have my children with me.

Now, ten years on, I have witnessed first-hand the incredible impact of outdoor learning —children forming lasting friendships, challenging themselves, gaining confidence, and returning year after year. This chapter explores the power of time spent in the woods and how it can shape children and give them lifelong tools to help them navigate this world.

The origins of Forest School can be traced back to Scandinavia in the early 1950s, rooted in the concept of *Friluftsliv*, which translates to 'open-air living'. In Denmark, a woman named Ella Flautau began taking her own children, along with her neighbours' children, into the local woods for an informal kindergarten experience. The children were encouraged to set their own agendas, explore nature, and engage in activities such as outdoor cooking and storytelling. This approach quickly gained popularity among parents, leading to the widespread adoption of outdoor learning for children under seven across Scandinavia.

Educational theorists like Maria Montessori and Jean Piaget, who championed experiential play and hands-on learning in natural environments, laid the foundation for what would later become the Forest School movement. However, it wasn't until the early 1990s that students, inspired by the Danish preschool system, introduced the concept to the UK, where it rapidly gained traction.

Recognising its benefits, the Forest School Association was established in 2012 to provide formal recognition and set high standards for Forest Schools.

The Forest School ethos is built upon six key principles:

1. Regular sessions, ideally held weekly, with the same group of learners over an extended period.

2. Outdoor learning in a woodland or natural setting, allowing direct interaction with nature.

3. A child-led approach that encourages exploration, discovery, and supported risk-taking.

4. Leadership by qualified practitioners trained in child development and outdoor learning.

5. A holistic approach to education, fostering social, emotional, physical, spiritual, and intellectual growth.

6. The promotion of resilience, independence, and confidence through supported self-led challenges.

In my experience, running my own Forest School with these principles in mind has shown remarkable results. Children who struggle within the confines of a traditional classroom environment often thrive in the woods. The combination of freedom and clear boundaries allows their creativity to flourish, enhances self-regulation, and boosts self-esteem as they take on challenges and experience success.

Research suggests that Forest Schools have a profound impact on child development, fostering confidence, social skills, language, communication, motivation, concentration, physical abilities, and overall knowledge. Additionally, children promote a deep connection with nature and this enhances overall wellbeing. Studies indicate that exposure to natural environments is particularly beneficial for children, as it stimulates creativity, imagination, and cognitive development while strengthening social relationships. In green spaces, children tend to engage in more imaginative and creative play compared to traditional indoor settings.

From my own observations, I've noticed that after an initial session — where children are often a little 'wild' as they adjust to the new environment — their ability to empathise and show kindness begins to develop naturally. They become more comfortable working in teams while also demonstrating improved concentration and independence in their individual activities. Some of the most magical moments I've witnessed occur when the entire forest falls silent — not out of instruction, but because each child is so deeply immersed in their own task, completely unaware of what others around them are doing. These moments of deep-level learning highlight the powerful, transformative effects of Forest School.

It's all well and good to talk about the benefits of outdoor play and the transformative experiences children can have in nature — every story I've shared is absolutely true. But as a parent, I also understand that real life often throws up hurdles that make it difficult to create these ideal moments. Whether it's time constraints, resistance from your child, or simply not knowing how to make the most of these experiences, it's not always as easy as it sounds.

So, how can you help your child truly benefit from the time you spend outdoors together? As well as being a Forest School leader, I'm also an NLP practitioner, hypnotherapist, and Time Line Therapy® practitioner, specialising in helping children break free from limiting beliefs. Over the years, I've seen first-hand how small mindset shifts can make a huge difference in how a child engages with the world around them. By understanding how to support your child emotionally and mentally, you can open the door to deeper learning, greater resilience, and more meaningful connections with nature — and each other. However, encouraging empathy, kindness, and a deep connection to nature in our children is only truly possible when our own mindset is in the right place.

I've come to realise that parenting is one of the hardest things we'll ever do. It's a constant balancing act — feeling the need to set firm boundaries while wondering if we're being too harsh, questioning whether challenging behaviour stems from something deeper at school, and replaying throwaway comments we regret. The emotional load can feel endless.

But then, I had my biggest lightbulb moment...

We've all heard the phrase on airplanes: 'Fit your own oxygen mask first.' I never really thought much about it before, but now I see it as a perfect metaphor for parenting — and life. When we take care of our own mindset, nurture our ability to empathise, and create space to truly see and understand our children, we gain the energy and emotional capacity to facilitate meaningful experiences — ones they will engage with wholeheartedly.

So, before we dive into creating these magical moments outdoors, let's remember to breathe, reset, and give ourselves grace. Because when we are grounded, our children thrive. Looking after yourself isn't a luxury, as I used to think — I've come to realise it's essential.

I have so many wonderful tools to help both you and your child feel more in control. Here are some powerful yet simple exercises to help you and your child reset, build resilience, and create a sense of balance:

1. **Reframing Negative Self-Talk**

We all have moments when we speak to ourselves harshly—but what if you could flip those thoughts and take away their power?

Try this:

- Write down a few negative statements you often catch yourself saying.

    - *'I'm so stupid.'*

    - *'I have no support.'*

- Challenge them by finding evidence to the contrary.

    - Are you really stupid? When have you shown moments of intelligence, creativity, or problem-solving?

- Have you ever received support from someone in the past? Who could you reach out to now?
- Flip the script! Rewrite each statement in a more empowering way.
  - *'I have made mistakes, but I am learning and growing.'*
  - *'I have people who care about me, and I can ask for help when I need it.'*

By actively challenging these beliefs, you weaken their grip and shift your focus toward the positive truth. It's such a simple but transformational practice — try it and see how it changes your perspective.

2. Daily Affirmations

Train your brain to replace old, limiting beliefs with positive ones. Try this:

- Write down five things you like about yourself.
- Repeat them out loud daily for a week.
- The next week, pick a new five!

By consistently reinforcing these positive truths, you're rewiring your brain for greater confidence and self-worth.

3. Creating a Safe Space

When emotions run high, having a safe space to retreat to can help both you and your child self-regulate. This could be:

- A cozy corner in your home with cushions, books, or a soft blanket.

- A special spot outside — maybe under a tree or in a garden.

- A visualised safe space (for younger kids, this could be an enchanted forest or a superhero hideout!).

Encourage your child to design their own space and decide what makes it feel calming and safe. This gives them a tool for emotional regulation that they can use for life.

4. Square Breathing for Instant Calm

This simple breathing technique can quickly reset your mind and body.

- Breathe in for a count of 3, 4, or 5 — imagine drawing one side of a square.

- Hold for the same count — draw the second side.

- Breathe out for the same count — draw the third side.

- Hold again — complete the square.

Repeat a few times, and you'll feel more grounded, clear, and calm.

An NLP principle I remind myself of daily is that all we can do is use the tools we have available to us at the time, and that we are more than our behaviour. On particularly challenging days, kindness — to yourself and others — goes a long way. And if in doubt, get yourself outside.

Spending time outdoors offers a powerful reset, and nature provides all the tools you need. Try making your own clay by mixing sticky mud with a little water and dry earth, then sculpt woodland faces on trees as protectors of the forest. Gather natural items of varying colours to create patterns or sculptures, or build dens — whether for woodland fairies or for you and your child! These simple yet engaging activities not only spark creativity but also strengthen bonds, encourage teamwork, and bring a host of mental and physical health benefits.

Spending time outdoors isn't just about getting fresh air — it's about creating moments that shape a child's confidence, resilience, and connection to the world around them. I've seen first-hand how children thrive in nature, developing social skills, problem-solving abilities, and a deep sense of wonder simply by being allowed to explore freely. Whether it's making woodland faces from clay, building dens, or watching a trail of ants at work, these small experiences stay with them long after childhood.

As a child, I was lucky enough to roam the South Downs, climbing trees and immersing myself in nature, and those memories have never left me. I want to encourage you to give your child the same opportunity. It doesn't have to be complicated — just stepping outside, noticing the world together, and letting them play freely can have a lasting impact. In doing so, you're not only helping them build resilience and emotional wellbeing, but you're also giving them something priceless — memories that will stay with them for a lifetime.

Dedication:

To my boys, who have often shown me the error of my ways and inspired me to be the best mum I can be. You have taught me patience, resilience, and the true meaning of unconditional love. My greatest hope is that you walk through life grounded, confident, and always knowing your worth.

Biography:

Lucy Fenwick is a retired teacher with over 25 years of experience, an NLP practitioner, and a hypnotherapist specialising in helping children overcome anxiety-related challenges. She is also a Forest School teacher, running her own small business — now celebrating its tenth year — where she combines her passion for nature with child-led learning.

As a mum of two, Lucy understands first-hand the struggles of raising a child with anxiety and school-related challenges. Her own journey of self-discovery recently led to a self-diagnosis of ADHD, helping her reframe years of self-criticism and find new strategies to overcome challenges. This has deepened her empathy and drive to support others on similar paths.

Through her work, Lucy provides life long, practical tools for children and parents navigating anxiety, self-esteem issues, and school struggles. Could she be the guide you've been looking for?

You can connect with Lucy here:

https://linktr.ee/Happydayswithlucy

Putting Children First

Reducing the Harm of High-Conflict Divorce By AJ Gajjar

'The more healthy relationships a child has, the more likely they will be to recover from trauma and thrive. Relationships are the agents of change and the most powerful therapy is human love.' — Dr. Bruce Perry

Being a parenting and trauma consultant, I have spoken with many parents who feel stuck.

Stuck in feelings of guilt and shame because they just can't seem to co-parent well.

Stuck in feelings of helplessness and hopelessness because no-one seems to understand their experience or the experience of their children — not even professionals within the system who these parents once believed were there to help, support, and protect them.

Instead, they find themselves being told to continue to co-parent. To put their own differences aside and find a way to co-parent. Because co-parenting offers the best long-term outcomes for children of divorce.

Yet that is somewhat of a blanket statement with little to no consideration for the nuances of their circumstances. Nuances such as a history of domestic abuse. Of a current experience of post-separation abuse. The challenge of having experienced immense harm themselves at the hands of the individual they are now being told to co-parent with.

The truth is that co-parenting does, in fact, offer the best long-term outcomes for children of divorce.

That is what the research shows, and I stand by it.

The key, however, is that it needs to be *healthy co-parenting*. Healthy, in terms of both parents' psychological and emotional wellbeing, and both parents holding the best interests of their children as the utmost priority.

Healthy co-parenting is defined by what I call the 4 C's: Cooperation; Collaboration; effective Communication; and Common ground. The common ground being the best interests of your children.

What happens, though, when one parent is NOT psychologically or emotionally healthy? When one parent is high-conflict, has a personality disorder, is abusive, struggles with addiction, or is relationally complex and is either unwilling or just does not have the capacity to co-parent?

Well, for starters, you have NONE of the 4 C's.

Instead of Cooperation and Collaboration, you will have constant pushback.

Instead of effective Communication, you will have endless circular emails going back and forth for months, with no forward movement on any decision meant for the wellbeing of the children.

And you will have zero common ground. You, as the healthy parent will be operating from a place of what is in your child's best interest, while the other parent will be operating from a place of whatever is in *their own* best interest.

There is NO meeting in the middle.

Given this reality then, what can you possibly do to protect your children? When you've tried to co-parent for months, sometimes years, and tried everything you can to establish a healthy co-parenting relationship for the sake of your children, but through no fault of your own, nor for lack of trying, still can't seem to find a way. When friends, family, legal professionals, therapists — when *everyone* is telling you to co-parent, but you just can't seem to get it to work, what then?

Well, for starters, let me be the one to give you permission to *stop* trying to co-parent.

Yes, you read that correctly. STOP trying to co-parent.

Because here's the thing. If you keep trying to co-parent with someone who does not have the capacity to, you are actually causing more harm to your children. Your energy is focused on the conflict, thoughts, actions, and triggering reactions of the other parent and not on your children.

For example, how insulting is the next email going to be? How can I ask for what our children need and frame it in a way that doesn't make the other parent angry? What language can I use to make sure they understand the gravity of the situation at hand?

And while you're trying to manage the reactions and feelings of the other parent, you're distracted and not present with your children.

Due to their own challenges, the other parent is also not present, also not able to meet the needs of the children, and oftentimes due to the maladaptive and coercive parenting approach they implement, are causing these children overt harm.

How do I know your children are experiencing harm from coercive parenting?

Let me put it this way... if you were in a domestically abusive relationship, are currently in the midst of a high-conflict divorce, or are experiencing post-separation abuse, then there is a high likelihood that your children are experiencing coercive parenting.

Coercive parenting is a parenting approach that uses fear, intimidation, power, and control to obtain obedience from children, with little to no regard for children's emotional or psychological wellbeing (*International Journal of Environmental Research and Public Health, 2020*).

In an ideal world, you would be able to appeal to professionals within the family law system to help keep your children safe, and this system would acknowledge the emotional and psychological harm your children are experiencing. However, the current legal system is one that consistently prioritizes parental right over and above child safety, often leaving children in harmful environments for extended periods of time.

If that is the unfortunate reality of what you and your children are experiencing, what can you possibly do to protect your children despite the time they spend with the maladaptive parent?

For starters, you can learn to parent *differently*.

You can parent in a way that is responsive to the needs of your child. In a way that is child-centric, and rooted in empathy, compassion, support, and connection. In a way that is rooted in relationship. A relationship that will be *the most important* factor that protects your children from the long-term damage caused by their experience of ongoing trauma.

Trauma doesn't have to be one single, significant, life-altering event. It can be. But it doesn't have to be.

In these circumstances, the trauma is more ongoing. Small, subtle experiences that the child has and internalizes which, as Dr. Dan Siegel says, 'overwhelms their capacity to cope'.

It is 'ongoing' trauma, because as long as these children are spending time with the maladaptive parent, these children will continue to experience harm at the hands of that parent.

Consistently having their feelings dismissed or invalidated, feeling unseen, unheard, ignored, and like they don't belong — causes trauma. Comments heard consistently such as '*Stop your fake crying, there's no need to be so upset, go to your room and come out when you're ready*', can over time erode a child's sense of self-worth and self-esteem.

Coercive parenting also frequently involves the consistent undermining of the child's relationship with the protective parent. Hearing things like '*Your mom doesn't really love you like I do*' or, '*I'm so sorry Mommy works so much and doesn't have enough time for you*', causes an immense amount of confusion and emotional disruption to a developing child.

This ongoing emotional and psychological harm children experience can lead to significant negative long-term outcomes on their psychological, emotional, and even physical health — IF there are no interventions.

Which is why it becomes vitally important for you, the protective parent, to provide that intervention. Parenting children who are experiencing maladaptive and coercive parenting is unlike any other. The trauma these children are experiencing is undermining and stalling the healthy growth and development of their brains, and hence these children have unique developmental needs. Needs that can be addressed through parenting in a way that involves helping them process their experiences and releasing their emotions from the time spent with the maladaptive parent, and in a way that helps them heal the trauma they have experienced.

So, how exactly can you, the protective parent, *heal* your child's trauma?

Through your relationship.

Trauma occurs in isolation. It heals through relationship.

One of the first things, and one of the hardest things you can do to heal your child's trauma, is to shift your focus away from what the other parent is or is not doing. Get crystal clear on what you can and, more importantly, what you CAN'T control, and focus your time, attention, and energy on the things that you can influence. Like being truly present and emotionally attuned to your children.

Remember, there is no amount of communicating, negotiating, yelling, playing nice, or prescribing that is ever going to change anything the maladaptive parent does or doesn't do. So, there is ZERO point in wasting any time or energy on that.

It is far more effective to be present and responsive to the needs of your child.

One thing that can help you to show up in the way your children need you to, is your own self-care. Now, before you roll your eyes at something you have likely already heard and heard again, let me explain.

When your children return home to you, they are likely dysregulated from being in an environment that they haven't felt fully comfortable in. If they are dysregulated, they will need you to help them regulate. And this is not something you will be able to do if you yourself are dysregulated.

Prioritizing your own self-care, during times when your children are not with you, is essential in supporting this process. At the risk of using an already overused analogy, you must put your own oxygen mask on first before you can put one on your child.

Self-care doesn't have to be about manicures and bubble baths and spoiling yourself. In circumstances where you, as a parent, have found yourself to be deeply hurt, confused, and traumatized, self-care is deeper than a warm bath and reading a book. It is about finding a sense of peace and calm. About eating healthily, sleeping well, and drinking lots of water. About finding your own rhythm and joy again. About grounding and finding your way back to yourself. It is about taking care of yourself.

The next step, after you get yourself to a place of relative calm, is for you to help your children return to their own sense of calm. To return to a sense of safety.

Safety in this context is not about physical safety. It is not about having a warm bed, a living space without hazards, and food on the table — although that is part of it. Safety in this circumstance is all about emotional and psychological safety. These children need to feel safe in your presence and in the environment you create for them.

That kind of safety is created through stability in your own emotional affect and responses, as well as through environmental consistency and predictability.

Your children need to know what to expect when they return home to you. What kind of mood you will be in, how you will behave, and how you will react if they tell you something that is challenging to hear.

It is also important to maintain consistency and predictability in their physical environment. Ask them what they would like to have for dinner and have that ready for them. Have their bedrooms untouched from when they left. Do what you can to make sure the house smells and looks the same as the last time they saw it.

The majority of children experiencing coercive parenting struggle with change. They feel like they have no power, control, or agency when they are with the maladaptive parent. Seeing things changed in their home while they were gone can increase their feelings of lack of control and contribute to their dysregulation.

Your home — the protective parent's home — needs to be one that encourages calm, stability, and predictability — not further dysregulation.

It is this feeling of emotional and psychological safety that will help your child's brain heal. The brain is an amazing organ and has an immense amount of neuroplasticity (ability to reorganize, rewire, and heal). Your primary job as the parent is to create and provide the optimal environment for your child's brain to feel safe in. Once it feels safe, it will resume development and start the healing process all on its own.

Of course, despite your best efforts, you are not going to get it right 100% of the time. You're only human, after all — and that is where the importance of repair and reconnect comes in.

Being honest and making repairs with your children after a rupture is crucial to maintaining a sense of safety within the relationship. It is also important in allowing the relationship to grow and evolve. A rupture could be anything from a minor disagreement to a major misunderstanding. Ruptures occur in all relationships and are a completely normal part of the human experience. Therefore, ruptures do not inherently cause harm. What causes harm is when there are frequent ruptures which are left unaddressed, or with little to no effort made at repair.

Apologizing to children when their feelings have been hurt or they have been misunderstood, having a conversation around the fact that you recognize you could have reacted differently and will try to do different next time, are all efforts at repair.

You can admit that you are not perfect and that even as an adult you sometimes still make mistakes. It gives you the opportunity to model the importance of apology in a way that normalizes making mistakes and helps foster the development of a healthy growth mindset.

A critical learning for these children in particular is in recognizing that it is perfectly alright to have big and sometimes messy emotions, within the context of a *healthy and safe relationship*. It is during these times of repair that we can guide our children in recognizing the difference between what healthy and unhealthy relationships look like.

However, parenting in this kind of a child-centric, responsive, trauma-informed manner is not your normal style of parenting, and it can be extremely uncomfortable at first. Especially if it is completely different from how you yourself were raised, or compared to any ideas you may have held about how you would parent one day.

It is also not the kind of parenting that your friends or family may understand. But it is the kind of parenting these children *need*. Mainstream approaches to parenting are based on what could work when raising 'typically developing' children. I say 'could' work because even typically developing children have individual differences, making them respond differently to any given parenting style. So, there is a certain amount of trial and error required to land on the precise variation of the style that works effectively for any child.

Your children, however, are anything but typical. They have experienced coercive parenting and immense trauma. Their daily experiences are different. Their developmental trajectories are different. In fact, mainstream parenting approaches will not only *not* work for these children but can further perpetuate the harm they experience and also damage their relationship with you, their safe parent.

Their relationship with you, the safe parent, is not one they can afford to lose. After all, there is only one person in the world that can heal your child's trauma in the most effective and efficient way possible. That one person is not a doctor, psychologist, or counsellor.

That one person is YOU.

Dedication:

To all the children experiencing harm from high-conflict divorce and coercive parenting: I see you. I hear you. You are not alone.

Biography:

AJ Gajjar is a mom, parenting and trauma consultant, child development specialist, and children's advocate. She supports concerned parents to protect and empower their children not only to recover from trauma, but also to develop resilience against future traumas.

AJ also supports professionals within the domestic violence, family law, children's mental health, and child protection sectors to recognize the detrimental effects of high-conflict divorce on children.

Throughout AJ's career, she has focused on improving long-term outcomes for children. Over time, her attention shifted to the impacts of divorce on children and she became increasingly interested in the dynamics of high-conflict divorce and coercive parenting that often comes with it. That is when AJ decided to combine her education in developmental psychology and over 18 years experience in early childhood development and mental health to create Trauma Healing

Parenting – a parenting model specifically designed to best support children who experience the impact of high-conflict divorce and ongoing relational harm.

You can connect with AJ here:

https://linktr.ee/ajgajjar

Why Food Matters in Mental Health
By Lucy Harper

'All diseases begin in the gut.' — *Hippocrates, 460-370BC*

Our health care system is broken, and it won't be 'unbroken' until we have a different approach to health. We have virtually eradicated contagious diseases, but those related to lifestyle are increasing at a rate of knots and becoming more complex. Unless we start looking downstream, we will not know how to fix people. We have an allopathic medical system that compartmentalises conditions and simply tries to put a plaster on the disorder without looking at possible underlying causes, be it with physical or neurological issues.

An example of this is a young girl I worked with. Rosie was 15, depressed, constantly exhausted, losing her hair and eyelashes. She regularly fainted and had numerous gut issues. She'd been written off by two hospital consultants as having 'functional bowel disorder' and told that it was something she'd always have so might as well just get used to it. Fortunately, Rosie's grandmother had consulted me regarding her own gut issues a few years prior to my meeting Rosie. I remembered her well because she'd broken both her ankles on a walk, for no reason.

What could cause such brittle bones in a woman who was in her early fifties? The most likely cause is lack of nutrient absorption due to gut inflammation triggered by a food. Just that bit of awareness of Rosie's family history was enough for me to see gluten as the red flag. Rosie didn't have Coeliac Disease, according to the tests carried out by the hospitals, but these tests are limited, and false negatives are high. Within days of adopting a gluten-free diet, Rosie was feeling much better, and within three months all her symptoms had gone. Undoing all those years of food being associated with pain was the hardest part of her recovery.

I had become very interested in the link between what one ate and health concerns due to issues in my immediate family. My daughter, although an unusual case, is by no means as rare as the medical profession appears to believe. When she was around 15, she felt things were out of her control. Her best friend was suffering severe mental health issues. My daughter felt she'd let her down, because she couldn't prevent her friend from becoming a school refuser, nor from spiralling into self-destructive behaviour. As a result of the pressures, my daughter started to self-harm, became depressed and very anxious. Despite having a lovely set of friends, she didn't feel connected with any of them. School wasn't the problem, as she enjoyed the work, was an A-star student, and hadn't missed a single day for years. But now she, too, was at risk of becoming a school refuser.

When she told me the voices in her head were becoming sinister and her visualisations more frequent, I realised just how serious the situation was. First port of call was to see the GP for basic tests as well as for Coeliac Disease (CD), as I knew CD could be a factor in mental health. Fortunately, I was halfway through my Nutritional Therapy

Master's degree and knew what private tests to do whilst waiting for the GPs test results to come back and which I was pretty sure would all report as 'normal'. I ran a gut permeability test which clearly indicated 'leaky' gut; this means that the tight barrier in the gut is allowing toxins through the gut wall that shouldn't go through, triggering several inflammatory markers. Another test carried out to understand why her sleep was so poor revealed a cortisol spike mid-afternoon, as well as an elevated salivary immune marker to gliadin — a marker for immune activation against gluten.

These were simple tests, but they gave us the information we needed: gluten was highly likely to be an issue. The GP initially 'forgot' to test for CD (I don't think she took the request at all seriously and thought I was simply an 'over-anxious mum'), so we had to wait a few weeks longer before my daughter embarked on a strictly gluten-free diet. It was my daughter's decision to experiment with cutting out all grains. We introduced a gut repair protocol alongside the changes in diet, and within seven weeks the depression, anxiety, poor sleep, and the visual and auditory hallucinations, all disappeared. Time to go back to school and no anxiety. The black cloud of worry that hung over the family lifted.

What is interesting about these two cases is that both presentations were very different, but both had gluten as the underlying issue, resulting in gut permeability and inflammation. There are hundreds of papers on Non-Coeliac Gluten Sensitivity (NCGS), including my own, and most doctors are at last recognising NCGS as a possible cause in Irritable Bowel Syndrome (IBS). Unfortunately, though, they rarely question diet when presented with a patient with a mental health issue. For every patient who presents with gut issues related to gluten intolerance, eight will present with symptoms that are not associated with the digestive system.

Gluten, as found in wheat, barley, and rye, is the most problematic food. If it is suspected that gluten foods are an issue, it's important to rule out Coeliac Disease, which requires strict adherence to a gluten-free diet. Symptoms of CD, just like NCGS, can include depression, brain fog, ADHD-like behaviour, and any number of other inflammatory symptoms. It should also be noted that high levels of fructans in wheat and other foods can be a cause of gut issues, but this will not be causing mental health issues.

Studies involving IgG testing have found other allergenic foods to be a factor in depression for some young people, as well as in Attention Deficit Hyperactivity Disorder (ADHD). The most common foods which study participants were reacting to were found to be eggs, dairy, soya products, seafood, nuts, mustard, sesame, celery, sulphur dioxide, and sulphites. Following testing, participants experienced significant improvements in depression by eliminating the foods which indicated a high positive in the test.

Often you can have an intolerance to a food without being aware that it is affecting you — until you eliminate it!

However, that doesn't mean I'd recommend rushing out to do a food intolerance test, for the simple reason that the market is inundated with rather dubious tests and false claims. You need to know what to test for, how to reliably test for it, and which analysis will give you useful and applicable information. You also need to be aware of if and how you should reintroduce the eliminated foods.

The reason why foods can trigger mental health symptoms is that any food that triggers an immune or an inflammatory response can affect the microbiome and the brain. A high sugar/carbohydrate diet creates blood sugar imbalance. This increases cortisol, adrenalin, and other hormones, and leads to a rollercoaster in blood sugar levels.

Over time it impacts the gut microbiome and increases anxiety and irritability.

The health of the gut microbiome is critical to both physical and emotional wellbeing. A disruption to the composition of the bacteria can play havoc, as clearly illustrated by what happened to my other daughter.

When she was 13, she seemed to suddenly change personality. From being a lovely, bubbly child, she became aggressive and generally horrid to be around. I began to wonder whether I could put her up for adoption, but who would want such a child? I reminded myself of how special she had been as a toddler (don't all mums think their kids are special?). So, what had gone wrong? We are a very close family who love to chat and just be together. Having a psychotherapist in the family means talking is what we do.

I started to wonder about testing, but I didn't know where to start until, just by chance, we found out that she'd been buying lots of junk food and sugar-laden drinks from school. I wondered if that could be a cause for the change in behaviour. And to find that out, I knew what test to carry out! We ran an Organic Acid test — a urine test that measures 72 different metabolites. It indicated a high candida (a yeast overgrowth) score and low levels of certain neurotransmitter metabolites. This time it wasn't gluten that was the culprit but junk food!

Fortunately, the yeast overgrowth hadn't had time to get a good hold, and we were able to eradicate it very quickly and improve the levels of feel-good neurotransmitters. Within no time at all, her aggressive behaviour ceased, and she was back to her lovely, happy self.

Looking at the research, it has been shown that there is a strong correlation between candida and bacterial overgrowth and mental health. We all have a certain level of yeasts (our mycobiome) in our gut, with the most abundant being *Candida tropicalis.* But like all the bacteria in our gut microbiome, it needs to be in balance. The bi-directional communication between the gut and the brain is critical to our central nervous system.

Over 70% of our neurotransmitters, such as serotonin, dopamine, and GABA, are produced in the gut. Serotonin is critical to mood, and to the ability to cope with anxiety and stress. This is the neurotransmitter that most anti-depressants aim to increase. All our neurotransmitters need to be in balance, and this requires the correct nutrients and a healthy microbiome to support nutrient bioavailability. Our gut bacteria synthesise 'B' vitamins and other nutrients and are actively involved in the body's ability to utilise nutrients.

Research papers invariably show that those living with mental health conditions have a significantly less diverse microbiome. They have also been shown to have fewer short-chain fatty acid-producing bacteria, which are critical to physical and emotional health, and for the bacteria to be more pro-inflammatory.

As was reported in the media in 2024, a staggering two-thirds of calories consumed by 11-to-18-year-olds comes from ultra-processed foods (UPFs). This is a particularly worrying trend, as these youngsters are in their formative years, when habits can become ingrained. Perhaps even more worrying is that one-in-four children leaving primary school is obese, presumably because they are eating far too many over-processed foods. It's been shown that one-in-six children is living with a mental health issue, with an increasing number presenting with eating disorders.

Whilst government recommendations are five portions of fruit and vegetables a day, children eat on average less than half this. Their fibre intake is far too low, with only 4% meeting the recommended dietary guidelines. The intake of essential fatty acids (EFA), as found in oily fish, seeds, and nuts, is also only 25% of recommended guidelines. A deficiency in EFA can impact the brain and can increase the risk of weight gain, fatigue, depression, alcohol and food cravings, anxiety, insomnia, pain, Attention Deficit Disorder (ADD), and ADHD. Healthy fats are essential for the absorption of certain essential vitamins, such as vitamin A, D, E, and K, and to produce neurotransmitters.

More than 20% of 11-to-18-year-old girls are deficient in vitamin A, in riboflavin (B2), iron, calcium, magnesium, iodine, selenium, and zinc. We often also see deficiencies in folate (which increases the risk of anaemia), vitamin D, and potassium. Adhering to a vegan or vegetarian diet can increase the risk of nutritional deficiencies, unless it is well thought out. Because of the high levels of anti-nutrients, such as phytates, lectins, and other compounds which are plants, seeds, and grains' natural defence mechanism, certain nutrients have a reduced bioavailability. This can increase the risk of vegetarians and vegans suffering from deficiencies.

Other reasons for nutritional deficiencies include the consumption of excess calories through ultra-processed food. These are pre-packaged sandwiches, pizzas, cereals, anything with refined oils, sugar, and carbohydrate-dense foods. It also includes margarines, as these are made with highly unnatural ingredients which have been sold to us as 'healthy' alternatives to butter. Refined oils such as sunflower and vegetable oils have been shown to cause cellular damage and have been described as a public health disaster.

Artificial colourants, benzoate preservatives, artificial sweeteners, and synthetic emulsifiers all have the potential to degrade the microbiome, increase inflammation, and thereby increase the risk of mental health disorders, including ADHD and behavioural conditions. We know that artificial azo food dye and sodium benzoates are toxic to the nervous system and cause behaviour issues in children, yet they are still included in foods aimed at children. Even commercially produced baby food is associated with food allergy in childhood, according to a systematic review of UPF published in 2024.

ADHD is the most prevalent psychiatric disorder in children and can present alongside anxiety, depression, learning disorders, or behavioural challenges. Whilst we may not know the exact causes of ADHD, we do know that food and food intolerance is often a factor. Iron, for instance, is a co-factor in the synthesis of dopamine. Both low iron and dopamine levels are often seen in those who have ADHD. Yet it doesn't mean supplementing iron will necessarily improve ADHD symptoms, because the issue could be in a lack of other co-factors. The full picture needs to be considered, and a proper evaluation of the diet needs to be made.

We live in symbiotic harmony with micro-organisms, and we need this bacterial world to remain in balance so that we may flourish. Bacteria live on our skin, in our body, and are most abundant in the digestive tract. A few hours before birth, the mother's vaginal micro-biome changes. This ensures that the newborn has been given a good dose of the right bacterial species to protect it from the micro-organisms to which it will be exposed through food and the environment. Beneficial bacteria help maintain a healthy gut and keep pathogenic bacteria, which produce toxins, in check.

We have an epidemic of children with 'funny or particular' feeding habits which we see develop as soon as solids are introduced. These habits often involve limiting foods to starchy, sweet foods, bread, and refined carbohydrates. Added to this are antibiotics, other medication, and stress, which can all be major factors in upsetting the careful balance of our microbial world.

So, what can you do to support your child's general and mental health?

Simple steps include:

- Swapping refined oils for healthy fats such as extra-virgin olive oil, butter, ghee, coconut oil.

- Changing processed snacks for seeds and nuts (avoiding salted peanuts!), dried fruits such as figs, dates, apricots (unsulphured).

- Wean off high-sugar-laden foods and drinks including synthetic sweeteners, which damage the gut microbiome.

- Avoid eating wheat foods more than once a day. Replace wheat with different grains such as buckwheat (which has nothing to do with wheat as it's from the rhubarb family), quinoa, teff (an ancient grain).

- Ditch table salt, which is pure sodium stripped of all the other beneficial minerals salt should contain. Swap for Himalayan pink salt or pure sea salt.

- Encourage children to eat as many different coloured fruit and vegetables. Eating 30 or more gut-supporting foods — be that fruit, vegetables, spices, herbs, wholegrains, healthy fats — encourages a more diverse microbiome and better physical and emotional health.

And finally, work with a registered professional to ensure your child's diet is right for them.

Aim for the rainbow!

Dedication:

To my daughters, Jessy and Tamzin, who have taught me so much.

References:

Link to Google docs for the list of references used in this chapter: https://bit.ly/4iUeJIx

Biography:

Lucy Harper is a British Association of Nutrition and Lifestyle Medicine (BANT) accredited Nutritional Therapist, Wellbeing Coach, and Emotional Freedom Technique practitioner. After years of teaching, traveling, and running a fair-trade business, Lucy then changed direction to follow her passion for health. This decision came about following the introduction of a little-known diet at that time, which was found to be very effective in alleviating symptoms in her husband. Over the course of her training, the passion for nutrition was reinforced by the experience of her children.

Since completing the Master's degree in Nutritional Therapy in 2016, Lucy has been supporting clients to reclaim their health. Further training has led her to specialise in supporting clients struggling with unexplained pain and fatigue, having trained with the Chrysalis Effect. Lucy went on to add Emotional Freedom Technique, which for some clients provides the missing key to health. Based in Bristol in the UK, Lucy sees clients both online and in person.

If you would like to work with Lucy and reclaim health for yourself or a loved one, find out more by going to the link below.

You can connect with Lucy here:

https://linktr.ee/lucyhealth

Nurturing Hearts
Meeting the Emotional Needs of Your Child By Keri Hartwright

'Behind every behaviour is a positive intention.'
(An NLP presupposition)

When a child's behaviour suddenly changes or they are very emotional, it is good to look at their emotional needs and what is happening in their lives. Their world is often relatively small, and a change in the home, school, or friendship circle can have a huge impact. In this chapter, I will focus on how, as parents, you can support your child to meet all their emotional needs. When these are being met, it improves mental health and overall wellbeing. I aim to give you some tools to share with your children, friends, and family, which will help you on your journey.

Over the years I have worked with many young people and their parents, supporting them with their mental health and acting as the adhesive to bind them together when things have become unstuck. I help parents to better understand and connect with their young person. In 2012, I embarked on my journey as a parent.

As a teen, I struggled with bullying and felt alone because I didn't know who I could talk to. I had returned to the UK from a life abroad, with my own personal trauma, and I didn't fit in at school. Many of my emotional needs were unmet, and my school journey was a lonely one. Sometimes as adults, the decisions we make can impact our child's emotional needs without any intent to cause distress. As an adult, I have seen the effect that poorly managed mental health can have on a whole family.

Children are not born with an instruction book, because each is unique and special, which can seem daunting to parents. What happens with one child, and how they respond, will be different for another. If we can support our young people with tools for a positive mental health when they are young, it will be invaluable as they reach adulthood and face life's challenges.

During adulthood, life can be a rollercoaster with ups and downs, twists and turns. Being able to manage these challenges and come up with practical solutions is an important skill set. As parents, we can support our children in developing these tools. Trying to clear their path of any obstacles or pitfalls can be tempting, though this doesn't reflect real life. Instead of giving them a clear path with no obstacles, we can provide them with a compass and show them how to use it to find their way.

Humans all have emotional needs. They also have the resources to meet their needs. Sometimes, when trying to meet a need, our child or young person may clash with us. For example, a child who dislikes school and refuses to get dressed in the morning is unlikely to be trying to upset you. They are more likely to be trying to take control of their situation. Ivan Tyrell and Joe Griffin from the Human Givens Institute identified our emotional needs as the Human Givens. When they are born, babies are totally dependent on their parents for all their needs. As they get older, they start trying to meet their own needs.

I will go into further depth about this subject with some ideas about supporting your child. Every living person has basic survival needs: to eat, sleep, and exercise. Ensuring our children have enough food to eat, a good regular sleep pattern, and some exercise daily, means they will have enough energy to get through the day, learning effectively and feeling well rested.

Exercise helps with focus, increasing blood flow to the brain and reducing the stress hormone cortisol. Once the cortisol level is lower, children are better able to learn, as they can take in new information more effectively. The fresh air and natural light help prepare for sleep at night as this resets the master clock. Regular exercise helps regulate emotions as stress hormones are lowered.

Sleep is vital for the healthy development of children, and its importance shouldn't be underestimated. But why is it so important? Sleep allows our children to grow, boosts energy, and puts the information they have taken in during the day into their memory store. It also helps lower levels of cortisol and supports emotional regulation. Children need to go to sleep at a regular time and get up at a regular time. The amount of sleep required slightly depends on age, but the recommended range from the age of three, right the way up to teens, is between 9 and 12 hours.

In the book *Why We Sleep*, the author Matthew Walker, cites a study at Harvard University which shows a direct link between memory and sleep in university students. In a controlled experiment, the students were 40% less able to remember facts they had learnt when deprived of sleep.

So, how can we help our children sleep better?

- Encourage a routine with some wind-down time before bed.

- Ensure they don't use screens too late into the evening/study too late, ideally with a gap an hour before bed.

- Offer them a snack before bed that contains tryptophan — an amino acid which helps the body produce melatonin — especially if they wake up hungry at night/early in the morning.

- Make sure the environment for sleep is as good as it can be, so not too hot or cold, low levels of light.

- If they are experiencing some worries, try to confine them to a chat separate from bedtime, as this may be when worries tend to surface. Put a notebook beside their bed for them to write down their thoughts.

As our children age, whilst they may be more independent, they will still need guidance around sleep and food. I have seen that teens can be more inclined to skip meals or choose unhealthy snack foods. They will also want to surf on social media/games/study late, impacting sleep quality.

In addition to our basic survival needs, we have emotional needs, which are to people what sun, water, and soil are to flowers. These include:

Security — feeling safe in the home, school, and environment is vital. Living/studying in an environment full of stress will impact a person's wellbeing. If you notice a sudden behaviour change, ask yourself:

1. Has something in their environment changed?

2. Are there difficulties with friendships?

3. Is there difficulty accessing the curriculum?

4. How are things in the home?

5. Have they had a new sibling come into the family?

6. Are there any difficulties in relationships at home?

Children can be sensitive to changes in their home environment, and a slight change in school or home can significantly impact their sense of security.

Emotional Connection — is a vital need. There has been a lot of research on attachment and how important it is. Everybody needs someone in their lives with whom they have a strong bond. It can be a close relative, if parents are not around. Regular physical contact when they are young, such as hugs, helps boost self-esteem and confidence. Spending 1:1 quality time with a child each week is a great way to build that emotional connection.

Some ways to build upon emotional connection with your child/children are as follows:

1. Regular screen-free mealtimes with the whole family, including at least one caregiver. If they eat early, sit and have a cup of tea while they are eating. This will encourage teens out of their room and generate conversation. It will allow you to learn about their day and build a family connection.

2. When they are young and playing a game, join in their game, build Lego with them, or play cars/dolls/make-believe/board games.

3. Read to them before bed each night. Stories are also a good way to help if they are struggling with some worries/friendship issues, for example.

4. If they are older, try a game night or a movie night.

5. If you have a dog, go out for a walk with them and the dog; sometimes sitting face-to-face can be a bit unnerving, and driving or walking can be less daunting.

Attention — we all need a balance of attention, so we need to both give and receive it. Children thrive on positive attention. If they don't get regular attention from you, they will act out or in a way you prefer to avoid, because some attention is better than none. And again, 1:1 positive attention is a good way to meet this need. If you have a lot of children, assign a time slot each week for each child. Try to notice their good behaviour and praise that. This will lessen the need to look for negative attention.

If you need to get chores done, involve them in your tasks. Then they will be with you, and you can still do what you need. To help them to give attention, get them to participate in random acts of kindness to those around them.

Control and autonomy — even when you start to wean them and they push the food out of their mouth, your child is trying to take control. Everyone needs control over the essential things in their life, but as a rule children often do not have much control. They get told what to eat, how to spend their day, what to wear, and what to do in school. Giving them control over simple things when they are young may reduce frustration and big emotions. For example, let them have choice over their clothes, or if this feels a bit tricky, giving them options for what to wear can make the process easier. I remember when my daughter was small, she used to wear the oddest combination of clothes, but allowing her the choice helped us leave the house promptly and developed her confidence. If a child has sensory needs, choice over clothes will be critical.

Privacy — having time and space to reflect on our day. Space to breathe and have some quiet helps us to regulate ourselves. If multiple children are in a bedroom, try to create a private space where they can be on their own now and then, if they need time. However, too much time alone is not a good thing, so if your teen is shutting themselves away regularly on their phone, make it a rule as they get older that even if they spend the rest of their evening in their room, they eat their food in the living area/kitchen/lounge rather than taking it upstairs. This will also improve your relationship with them, with regular contact in what can be an otherwise busy life. While it may seem that they want to be alone, sometimes they get lonely, though they don't know how to get out of this loop. As for privacy over their devices, this needs careful thought.

Connection to the broader community — research has shown that loneliness is a bigger killer than drugs or alcohol, and often in modern society, families are trying to manage things on their own. 'It takes a village to raise a child.' Being part of something helps us connect with others and reduces loneliness.

Friendships can be tricky to navigate growing up, and they are a large part of my conversations with young people in schools. Bullying, for instance, can be devastating to mental health. Friends are vital as young people try to find their identity; they help them find their place in society. As they age, they tend to move towards their peers more than their family. If they are part of a club such as guides/scouts/martial arts/swimming, separate from their school, they will meet other young people. This gives them options for friendships which are not isolated to school. The other young people will have shared interests, and they will also engage in activities that build their confidence and develop their social skills away from their phones/devices.

If you live far away from friends and family — as can be the case in big cities — getting connected to the broader community, such as a local charity or church, can benefit everyone. Our brains were designed to be part of a social group. And in times of crisis, such as war, our strength as a community has saved lives. These groups provide a support network for parents and extend the social circle of young people.

Achievement and competence — how to boost self-esteem is an essential subject for parents. Low self-esteem can have several roots, which may well start in childhood. This subject can be explored further with a suitably qualified counsellor if needed. As parents, we can help boost self-esteem by encouraging young people to achieve things for themselves. Get them to attempt things that are outside their comfort zone. One way to do this is to is to praise them for trying new things, rather than praising the results they get. If a child is a high achiever and used to getting good results, they may be less keen to push themselves to do more for fear of failure. Fear of failure is a real issue for many young people, and sports which are structured with rules will help them navigate this.

If we encourage them to try new things, they will learn new skills and find extra interests. As the skill set develops, this will help them see that they are achieving things, which builds on their self-esteem.

Team games can help with social skills as well. Involving them in clubs will give them a sense of achievement, especially if they do something like a competitive sport. If this doesn't appeal, allow them to solve their problems as they arise rather than giving them solutions. This can also be tied in with the need for meaning and purpose. Giving them responsibilities and achieving things for themselves will validate them and give them a meaning in life.

Respect — everyone likes to feel respected and heard. Giving your child a voice is important, so they feel valued. One idea is to have family meetings once a week, especially if things are unsettled in the house. This meeting will be a place to give everyone the chance to come up with one positive and one negative about the week. The meetings can start when they are young enough to have an opinion.

When it comes to setting boundaries, or disagreeing with them over a request they have which you are not ready to accommodate, having an open discussion where all viewpoints are heard will help them feel valued. The ultimate decision may lie with the parent, but feeling they were heard and getting to know your perspective may lessen the disagreement.

In conclusion, as parents we may be trying to balance out meeting the needs of everyone in the family, including ourselves. We might get it wrong sometimes, as it can be a bit subjective how we want our needs met. But it is also important for us to meet our own needs, or put our oxygen mask on first. Being aware of the emotional needs means you can take a step back when things are tough and see if you can find the reason behind the unwanted behaviour or emotional distress.

Dedication:

This chapter is dedicated to my daughter Emily. I am proud to join you as a published author. Thank you for being my inspiration every day.

Biography:

Keri Hartwright is a parent coach and counsellor, and director of a social enterprise. Her aim through her work is to reduce the stigma around mental health, reducing the effects of intergenerational trauma and giving people tools for life.

At 21, she qualified as a paediatric nurse, witnessing first-hand the struggles associated with having a sick child in the family. From there, her journey has taken her in many directions. She qualified as a school nurse in 2007, where she would hear the trials and tribulations of the day-to-day lives of young people, often which parents were unaware of. She acted as the glue to bring them back together.

This heightened her interest in mental health and led her to look for a more proactive way of managing mental health, rather than the reactive ways which exist within the NHS, so she trained as a Human Givens Therapist. Keri explained, 'When we go through life as a parent, our relationship with our child can become a little disconnected because of societal pressures, financial worries, work pressures, relationship changes, and much more. I am delighted to be a part of this book and hope it helps reduce the stigma of mental health, empowering the adults of the future.'

You can connect with Keri here:

https://linktr.ee/Kerihartwright

Compliance to Confidence

Nurturing Autonomy and Intrinsic Motivation Protects Young People's Wellbeing By Laura Linklater

'Perfection's a myth. There's only failing, then learning, then death.' —
Loto, Moana 2

This chapter will give you a sound base for understanding children's and adolescents' need for control and how you can support its development. I use *children* to refer to all those under 18.

Locus of Control and Autonomy

'Locus of Control' refers to how much control a person feels they have over their own life choices and behaviour. A person can either have an internal or external locus of control. Imagine using a compass to draw a circle — where you place the sharp point is the centre of this metaphorical locus.

Autonomy is the sense of independence or control of one's life trajectory. It is often introduced using the analogy of 'driving your own car'. If your locus of control is internal, you have a high degree of autonomy. If it is external, you tend to have a low degree of autonomy.

Reflection Point:

Consider the person who made you pick up this book and ask yourself:

1. Where is the centre of their Locus of Control right now?

2. What actions would help move that locus towards internal if needed?

3. How much autonomy do they feel they have?

4. What actions would help them feel they have a high degree of autonomy over their lives?

Motivation

Motivation is the driving force behind the choice to undertake an activity. We can further divide motivation into two types: extrinsic and intrinsic.

Extrinsic motivation refers to the desire to do something that originates outside the person doing it. Examples are, taking a job you hate for the money, doing something to avoid a negative consequence (e.g., missing playtime), or choosing a career because of other people's expectations.

Intrinsic motivation describes a desire to reach a goal that originates within the person. It requires a knowledge of one's values, preferences, and dreams, plus believing that they have the power to achieve their goal.

All three concepts dovetail greatly. An empowered person who knows themself and has an internal Locus of Control will feel a strong sense of autonomy and thus be guided by deep and positive intrinsic motivation. This combination of psychological safety and desire to complete their goals leads to what Maslow, in his Hierarchy of Needs, termed 'Self Actualisation'. It supports robust mental health and wellbeing, even when the inevitable setbacks are taken into account.

In contrast, having an external Locus of Control can lead to a disempowered person whose actions are guided by the needs and judgements of others, which can result in poor mental health outcomes.

If adults do not address these fundamental basics by taking action to change aspects of the child's environment (physical or psychological), they are unlikely to see a real change in their mental health, no matter how much mindfulness or breathing exercises they do.

The hidden costs of compliance in schools

Schools must find ways to balance behavioural standards and academic activity levels within the classrooms and corridors. This is even more challenging as class sizes balloon and budget constraints force headteachers to cut support staff.

The front line of teaching is exceptionally challenging. Most teachers are good, intelligent people trying their best with limited resources. However, many schools contain overwhelmed staff trying to get through the week by controlling behaviour and ensuring learning activities however they can. This results in an environment that emphasises obedience and conformity as virtues of the 'good student'.

On the flipside, an inability to express these virtues — most notably for SEND pupils, or perhaps those who are young in the year — labels a child as 'bad'. At the most charitable, teachers describe these children as presenting 'challenging behaviours'. Sadly, instead of supporting children to develop self-regulation, classrooms reward compliance as a short-term fix, which only compounds the issue.

Behaviour management is done in public, too, further chipping away at the child's sense of autonomy (and privacy). Younger years often employ some version of the traffic light behaviour system. Names written on a peg or a Velcro tag are moved up and down in a public display of how the teacher judges the child to be acting in class.

Essentially, the child is told, 'You are good: compliant'; 'not good: do better'; or 'bad: you are just being bad'. Schools can be very creative at using praise and shame to enforce compliance.

In addition to the pressure to comply with the school's behaviour policies, children and young people are constantly exposed to a culture of external validation. High-scoring children receive ticks and stickers in their books and are showered publicly with certificates during assemblies. The child who does not score seven-out-of-ten on their weekly spelling test (regardless of the reason) is to be seen sitting inside at playtime practising their mistakes.

The mental health toll of rigid school structures

Zero-tolerance discipline policies, uniform rules, and inflexible teaching methods carry a mental health toll on those who are subjected to them. It can feel oppressive in such a space day after day, particularly if it is hard for the child to adhere to the expected standards.

For neurodivergent or SEND students, sensory overwhelm, difficulty sitting still, or struggling with social expectations and interactions, let alone struggles which present an additional barrier to academic success, such as dyslexia, can make school an exhausting and even upsetting place to spend hours in every day. Their Locus of Control is very much in the hands of the school's adults.

In the high school years, a 'negative' [comment by the teacher] in the planner, which adds to previous notes, accumulates into missed opportunities or very publicly missing lessons to go into an isolation pod.

Aside from very public ability streaming for subjects in secondary school, I have sadly heard of several schools still publicly sharing test scores in termly class progress tests, or reading the numbers out during the register so that the students can write the score in their planners. And yet teachers continue to be frustrated with the question: 'Sir, is this going to be on the test?'

So, what are the effects of these practices on schoolchildren?

Disengagement

In the face of these highly structured, highly controlled, result-focused practices, many children become entirely disengaged. They disengage from their studies, from their daily school experience, and, in the long term, from their lives.

People-Pleasing

The stringent rules and blanket application to all students inevitably lead to children appeasing the teacher. Masking one's true identity or hiding one's struggles is especially true for SEND children, as any parent who has heard the depressingly familiar phrase, 'We are just not seeing it in school', will tell you.

Difficulty forming a strong sense of identity and self-worth

In the long term, this pattern of people-pleasing can make it difficult for children to form a strong sense of who they actually are. Many adults I work with in my Emotional Freedom Technique (EFT) practice speak of unpeeling the layers of people-pleasing fear to meet their true selves.

A young person who becomes dependent upon external sources to tell them what to do, what to study, and how and when to act, can also struggle with decision-making in adulthood. Understanding your authentic self does not magically take root after years of being held by others. It must be cultivated by those around the child so that they feel safe listening to and acting on their needs and wants for self-fulfilment.

Perfectionism and its friend Anxiety

Many bright children stop asking questions in class for fear of 'looking stupid'. They may even limit themselves to easier levels of work in class to be successful, fearing that pushing themselves will result in failure, which they cannot accept.

Schools often punish mistakes by forcing children to spend break time finishing work or correcting errors. They mark harshly in red pen or express disappointment at parents' evenings, further entrenching the idea that failure is shameful.

Unsurprisingly, many children develop a fear of failure and, for some (more often girls), a gnawing need to make everything perfect to avoid negative feedback and increase their chances of receiving affirming praise.

In secondary school, students begin to 'play the game' of studying only for the test, which is an excellent survival mechanism in such a results-driven environment but is a sad facsimile of what education should be. Many teens struggle with their sense of identity and self-worth being falsely equated with their grades and other external measures of success (such as having the lead role in the school play or taking on a leadership position in the school council). They suffer deep stress when they begin to struggle or bear the load of overcrowded revision timetables and pre-exam stress.

A fear of failure can lead to the triad of Perfectionism, in which students believe they must always succeed or risk feeling inadequate; Procrastination, the avoidance of tasks due to the fear of not meeting high expectations; and Burnout, pushing themselves too hard, leading to emotional exhaustion.

Checking Out

Those who know they cannot meet the expected levels check out entirely as their only means of protecting themselves psychologically.

In the words of one of my mentees, a Year 8 (12-year-old) boy with ADHD:

'I will never be the person to spin the rewards wheel in assembly. I have come to peace with that.'

Comparisonitis: The toxic cycle of measuring against others

The dangers of comparisonitis are well documented. Often, we hear about them in reference to social media, where real children encounter AI or filtered images of perfection that they cannot compete with. It is also hugely prevalent in schools, which foster an atmosphere of constant competition.

The insistence that students take a large number of GCSE courses, all of which they must excel in if they wish to attain praise and avoid failure, also presents students with the idea that they must be high achievers everywhere. It is entirely sensible when a young person then chooses not to take risks — even in subjects they love — to ensure the possibility of an A or a 7-9 grade.

This situation is anathema to following your interests. You cannot be risk-averse and also push the boundaries of learning at the same time. You cannot engage in out-of-the-box thinking while tailoring your education to what will be on the test.

The need for autonomy and flexibility

The late education expert and author Sir Ken Robinson asked us, 'Do Schools Kill Creativity?' in 2006. The more pressing question right now is, 'Do Schools Kill Motivation?'

Rigid, compliance-driven schooling discourages curiosity, creativity, and self-discovery. The external Locus of Control for students leads them to experience modern schooling as something that is done to them, not something they co-create with guidance and that serves their expression.

How parents and educators can foster intrinsic motivation

Here are some practical ways to encourage autonomy and self-directed learning in your child and work as a counterbalance, if needed:

Talk to them

Really, I mean 'listen to them'. Children may lack the verbal skills or confidence to discuss their feelings. It is up to us, the adults, to open the door and make it clear that they can talk to us about anything that weighs on them. We must invite them to the table (or sofa, or bedtime), and start the discussion. Some children — even older ones — need support to begin the conversation. Ask them about their experience of being a student at school and allow them to speak.

Is school the best place?

If your child is struggling with the school environment, consider whether it is the best place for them to learn. A parent or guardian has the legal duty to provide a suitable education for their child's needs. There are many options for providing your child with a comprehensive education that do not include mainstream schools, such as private school, EOTAS/EOTIS (Educated Other Than At/In School), Alternative Provision providers, and Elective Home Education.

Shift from external rewards to internal motivation

Alfie Kohn's book *Punished by Rewards* sets out in great detail the pitfalls of relying on excessive praise for our children. The crux of his work is that training our children to complete tasks in the expectation of rewards actually damages learning and drains motivation.

There is nothing wrong with telling your child you are proud of them. In addition, you can deepen their interest by asking open-ended questions that cause them to reflect on their love of their subject, such as, 'What was the most interesting thing you discovered today?'

Another great way to move from external validation to internal is to help children reflect on their progress and to celebrate effort, not just outcomes. You may tell them that you think their painting is excellent, then pick a feature and ask them a thoughtful question about it, such as, 'I love that you used red in the sun there as well as the yellow. What was your thought behind choosing that colour combination?'

Encourage self-directed projects

Even if your child attends school, you can set up project-based and child-interest-led projects to encourage autonomy and support your child's intrinsic motivation. This is one of the key features of the learning method known as Unschooling.

If you shared in the cultural conditioning that learning is something imparted through adults onto children, who are blank tablets awaiting instructions, it can be intimidating when your children's interests take them down a path about which you know little. You can use this as an opportunity to learn something new with them and demonstrate alongside them your learning process, including failing, adjusting (and re-adjusting), and trying again. This is one of the most powerful life lessons you can teach your child.

Allow for safe failure and problem-solving

You can show your child that failure is simply a stepping stone to a goal. Not only that, but it is entirely normal to fail multiple times on your path. You can search for examples of role models (fictional or real life) in which people have failed and learned, and discuss these with your child.

One great example is the Disney movie *Meet the Robinsons*, in which the family sits around the dinner table and asks, 'So, what did you fail in today?' They celebrate with cheers before asking what the next plan is.

More recently, the film *Moana 2* features an engineer, Loto, who is always seeking to improve her designs and often says to Moana: 'Perfection's a myth. There's only failing, then learning, then death.'

Another favourite is displaying a poster with the word FAIL as an acrostic for 'First Attempt In Learning'.

Reflection: Intrinsic motivation for life

Fostering intrinsic motivation and children's autonomy isn't a gimmick. Intrinsic motivation is key to both succeeding in life and enjoying yourself along the journey.

As with all aspects of parenting, we need to lead by imperfect example, trying, failing, adjusting, and being transparent about this process with our children. Every child deserves the opportunity to explore, create, and grow authentically — and so do their adults.

It's not just about education; it's about empowering a healthy mindset for a lifetime.

Dedication:

To all the children and young people who find school hard and who listen to their bodies and hearts, so that things can change and you can get the education you deserve. And to all the parents, carers, teachers, and adults who get it and who support them as best they can. Learning should feel safe. It shouldn't be this hard. I see you.

Biography:

Laura Linklater is an education consultant and specialist tutor with a deep commitment to empowering learners of all abilities. She is a qualified teacher with a Master's in Education, focusing on Equality and Diversity.

As the co-founder of The Motivated Learner, she provides academic support, SEND-specific tutoring, EOTAS provision, child mentoring, and guidance for parents navigating the complexities of education and mental health.

Laura specialises in neurodivergence-affirming education, ensuring that every student receives empathetic, tailored support that nurtures both academic success and personal confidence. She also advises on SEND legal matters and works with educators to create inclusive learning environments.

Passionate about fostering autonomy and intrinsic motivation in young people, Laura has developed *Trauma-Informed Educators* — an online course equipping parents and educators to support trauma-affected learners with confidence and care. She is a co-author of the Amazon number one best-selling book *Navigating Anxiety with Children and Teens*.

Through her consultancy, Laura advocates for educational approaches that prioritise student wellbeing, individual strengths, and long-term success. She works closely with families, schools, and professionals to reshape education into a more inclusive, supportive experience for all.

She lives in West Yorkshire with her husband, four home-educated children, and two cheeky guinea pigs.

You can connect with Laura here:

https://linktr.ee/themotivatedlearner

The Journey of Understanding and Being Empowered

from Behind the Mask of Neurodiversity, Eating Disorders, Mental Health, Suicide, Self-Harm, Trauma, and Other Life Experiences By Emily Nuttall

'Owning our story can be hard but not nearly as difficult as spending our lives running from it. Embracing our vulnerabilities is risky but not nearly as dangerous as giving up on love and belonging and joy — the experiences that make us the most vulnerable. Only when we are brave

enough to explore the darkness will we discover the infinite power of our light.' —— Brene Brown

Trigger warning: mentions sensitive subjects. I am not medically trained, so please see resources and helplines included in this chapter for support, or contact your GP.

Imagine your brain has just been thrown in a washing machine along with all the clothes, and it's in full spin cycle, churning round at its fastest speed. The different types and sizes of clothes represent your thoughts, voices of the anorexia and past abusers, feelings, emotions, behaviours, fears, sensory experiences, depression, anxiety, scary suicidal thoughts, self-harm, different traumas, and the voices of the emotional abuse you went through, neurodiversity, varying distress levels and life experiences. They're all jumbled up, struggling and unable to get around one another, becoming all tangled and twisted. The noise has become very loud and overwhelming to listen to.

You may be masking to try and show you're fine with it, or desperately trying to find a way to block out that noise and shut yourself down from it. Or maybe you're frantically trying to stop the washing machine in order to feel safe, process what is happening, and become grounded once again to find a sense of control. This is how the brain of an individual with these conditions and other life experiences, voices, and feelings can look and feel like.

As this has been me and my brain, I want to take you on a journey of unjumbling this washing machine brain and see that there can be a hopeful, helpful, healing way forwards for your loved one, with the right understanding, treatment, awareness, resources, love, care, compassion, and support.

Eating disorders

Research is still regularly being undertaken, but it is estimated that around one-in-five people who are neurodivergent are impacted by an eating disorder. This doesn't take into account those who are undiagnosed or being assessed for either neurodivergence or eating disorders, or both conditions, so the number is likely to be far higher.

The most common eating disorder types that relate to neurodiversity include anorexia, bulimia, binge eating disorder, Avoidant Restricted Food Intake Disorder (known as ARFID), and Other Specified Feeding and Eating Disorders (known as OSFED).

'Eating disorders are defined by abnormal eating behaviours that negatively affect a person's physical or mental health. These behaviours can include food restriction, binging, purging, and extreme exercising. Eating disorders often have underlying causes that may be related to mental health issues such as anxiety, depression, trauma, and perfectionism. For neurodivergent individuals, it is especially important to be aware of the signs and symptoms of eating disorders as they may present differently than in people who are neurotypical (a term used to describe individuals with typical neurological development or functioning). For example, some autistic individuals may demonstrate restricted food interests and limited meal patterns rather than the typical binge-purge cycle seen in other eating disorders. It is also important to note that neurodivergent individuals may not show the traditional signs of an eating disorder such as changes in weight or body shape, so the condition can go undiagnosed for long periods of time.'

(https://www.neddetraining.co.uk/post/eating-disorders-neurodivergence-often-go-hand-in-hand-here-is-what-you-need-to-know)

Shared neurodiversity and eating disorder traits

Neurodiversity and eating disorders link together in a variety of ways, in my experience. If you imagine a flower with its bud and nine petals, each petal represents a different element of their interlinking around the bud to bring the flower together with their shared traits, which include:

- **Masking** — this can be known as camouflaging and is a way to help shut down or disassociate from neurodiversity by carrying out eating disorder behaviours, whether that's restriction, binging, purging, or a combination, due to the high levels of energy needed to put on a front and be seen as able to function and cope. From my own experience, I was trying to show I was strong, managing, and needing a sense of protection, as well as an escapism from myself. And for me the anorexia would feed into that like it was my best friend and there for me.

- **Interoception** — this is where you can feel pain sensitivity, not being aware of hunger or satiety cues. Sometimes, neurodiverse people may experience pain with eating, or perhaps have a fear of choking on food and see certain food groups as a threat, causing them to avoid and restrict them, therefore reducing their intake of food groups as part of ARFID experiences. Others may not notice that they are hungry, which can cause the restriction, or may not notice their body's signals that they are full, resulting in bingeing. Others may continue to binge past the point of feeling full, as the discomfort of this 'over full' feeling can help soothe them, even if it results in causing them pain. If bingeing happens, the shame and guilt can feel like you're being crushed and cause purging episodes associated with bulimia. For me, it was almost like a fight, flight, or freeze response to my mind and body, and the anorexia would take advantage of that and stay terrifyingly in control of me through a cycle of the other eating disorder behaviours. But the restriction would still feel freeing and relieving.

Other petals include:

- **Emotional regulation challenges**. If you can't regulate emotions honestly, you may use food to block out, understand, relieve, or fill voids in emotions that may be missing.

- **Difficulties and overwhelm**, which causes trauma. And the other mental health challenges to feed in just add more anxiety and panic attacks.

- **Sensory experiences** such as distress with touch, smell, sight, and taste, causing food avoidance for ARFID and only building safe foods. Or with anorexia, it may enhance restriction, or with binge eating and bulimia you may binge more on these foods for the fear of losing them but purge because of the distress, guilt, shame, and uncomfortable feeling of pain. It can feel like you're trying to stop a big lump of jelly on a plate from wobbling really fast, and you may feel it in your body like jelly legs and be really shaky and panicky.

- **Rule-based thinking around food**, that it has to look a certain way, type, colour, or taste a certain way, and feel chewable to avoid the risks and fears of choking in ARFID experiences. Or you may present with a varied mixture of behaviours from different eating disorders to cope with these experiences (OSFED).

- **Need for routine, safety, and control**. Often avoiding social challenges and making social connections, as lots of these gatherings often involve food which, if not planned or prepared for, can be distressing and overwhelming.

- **Perfectionism.** Always feeling you need to be loved and good enough. This is something I can relate to from never feeling loved, valued, wanted, or good enough, and constantly like I was a labelled individual.

This brings the flower together.

How can we offer support?

- The blank canvas environment, giving control to help support treatment environments to be calm, grounding, safe, reassuring. This enhances empowering, trusting treatment connections to take place.

- Creative and alternative therapies to manage and motivate the mind, through art, music, play, and sensory toy therapies.

- The importance of embracing differences and diversities.

- Food and body sensory experiences.

- Being open-minded with a holistic approach.

- Understanding communication and engagement needs, through communication passports.

- Distress scales and traffic light systems. What is the level of distress before you engage? How can you effectively support with sensory and creative needs to reduce levels of distress and empower engagements?

- Support time and recovery outcome stars, and SMART (Specific, Measurable, Achievable, and Realistic goals set to a certain Timeframe).

- Understanding personality types.

- Suicide safety plans.

- Not losing hope.

The Do's and Don'ts

The importance of building routine and giving notice for any change as early as possible helped me to feel prepared and engaged and kept me able to cope with my treatment journey.

Consistency with care, treatment, and support from the professionals involved in supporting the individual, meant I didn't have to share my story again and again, so I did not become traumatised.

Systems for sharing information within the MDT (multi-disciplinary team) — autism, medical, and eating disorder teams — so that everyone knew what was happening.

Creative and alternative therapies, having things available to help me feel grounded and safe, and bringing items to treatment that helped to support, express, and cope with treatment. Examples of these include: art therapy, sensory toys, communication cards/passport, Lego therapy, playing instruments, dog therapy, and yoga, to name just a few.

For seeing me as an individual and not as a neurodivergent and anorexia diagnosis, or using labels for my other struggles and diagnoses. For walking alongside me, believing in me, and instilling the hope of recovery.

Be their connector, mentor, and guide, as together you can empower and inspire long-lasting change.

Exploring the 'I'm fine' Mask

My 'I'm fine' mask was like a ragged-haired, zoned-out, disconnected Emily staring back at me in the mirror, exhausted and shutdown. Wearing this mask of 'I'm fine' has blocked out distress, fear, trauma, flashbacks, health challenges, voices, devastating life events, helping me cope and understand my neurodiversity. It has guarded me from the pain, protected me from people's judgements, actions, and hurt, given me control, completely numbed me, and been a way to be able to disconnect and forget, yet still be this strong, smiling, determined, thriving, giving, achieving Emily for everyone around me in my life.

But underneath this mask has been so much more. Depression, anxiety, self-harm, suicidal thoughts, PTSD, autism, flashbacks, voices which then led to anorexia consumed both my mind and body in a terrifying and frightening way. But it felt like they were my best friends, as I never had the comfort, the safety blanket, and coping mechanisms I desperately needed. Instead, these feelings were there for me, would help make everything feel ok and get me through the trauma, turmoil, fear, pain, devastation, and loss of control that life had thrown my way. Unfortunately, though, this made it so much harder for me to be open and accepting of help and support, which prevented me accessing treatment.

I felt a lot of guilt and shame for being Emily. So, I had to be brave in various talking and creative therapies, to peel my mask back slowly like peeling off a plaster. And I needed to use my communication passport to engage in support. Finally, I had to learn to be my own patient, loving best friend, and to challenge that voice and empower Emily's voice to grow.

Where Am I Now on My Journey?

For me, my journey of experiences has been a recovery rollercoaster, full of ups, downs, twists and turns, loopdeloops, and steep drops. Healing is never a straightforward path, but I have become my own loving best friend. I am over a year self-harm free, have been in a sustained eating disorder and mental health recovery for 18 months, and have just celebrated seven-and-a-half years free of inpatient treatment.

I am truly empowering Emily in every way possible, bravely removing my 'I'm fine' masks, embracing, motivating, inspiring, and loving me for who I am as Emily. I am feeling it to heal it, facing everything and rising. And I have prevention, trigger, safety, and coping skill support plans in place. I describe it as a butterfly putting her wings together again and setting herself free, which is so beautiful, freeing, and healing. And it's a reminder that if I can do it, anyone can, because rock bottom became the solid foundation on which I rebuilt my life.

I am no longer ashamed of Emily, my experiences, or story, as these now empower and inspire others in all that I do. Without these experiences and expertise, I wouldn't have got to know the Emily I am today, the one I can love and can now empower other sufferers, professionals, families, carers, and others to tackle struggles with neurodiversity, eating disorders, mental health, suicide, and self-harm. And for that I will be forever grateful.

Helpful Links/Apps/Resources

https://www.beateatingdisorders.org.uk/get-information-and-support/about-eating-disorders/

There are a number of worthwhile links on this, including: types of eating disorders; getting help for myself/recovery; supporting someone else; early intervention; urgent support; e-learning platform; understanding recovery; asking for help; services for carers, etc.

https://beat.contentfiles.net/media/documents/gp-leaflet-website.pdf
https://beat.contentfiles.net/media/documents/beat-carers-booklet-1.pdf
https://www.peacepathway.org
https://prevent-suicide.org.uk
https://www.selfinjurysupport.org.uk
https://edacresearch.co.uk
https://www.kcl.ac.uk/research/eating-disorders-clinical-research-network
https://freedfromed.co.uk

Dedication:

I dedicate this chapter to everyone who is on a brave journey of healing, learning to understand and grow from their or their loved one's experiences of neurodiversity, eating disorders, and other mental health challenges, and for the professionals walking alongside them, believing and supporting them.

I would like to acknowledge Cassie Swift for being a truly wonderful, inspirational mentor and guide in helping me to complete my chapter. I couldn't have done this without your reassurance, understanding, guidance, and support.

I would like to acknowledge my trauma, mental health, eating disorder teams, counsellors, social workers, safeguarders, family support worker, and intervention teams, public protection officers, friends, family, my inpatient, day patient, outpatient treatment teams, surgeons, doctors, physiotherapist, occupational therapists, Action for Children, Grassroots Suicide Prevention, Victim Support, Self-Injury Support, Samaritans, NAPAC, Papyrus prevention of young suicide, and Beat, the UK eating disorders charity. And finally, all my colleagues in my paid and charity roles, who have been able to give me the opportunity to make long-lasting, positive changes and differences in care, support, services, and treatments in social care, education, autism, neurodiversity, disability, mental health, and eating disorders as an expert by experience. They have guided me, supported me, given me hope and strength in the darkness, protected me from harm, kept me safe, allowed my voice to be heard, allowed me to truly grow, and never given up on me.

You have all saved and changed my life for the better, reminded me that I am loved, worthy, and enough just as Emily. And for that I will always be eternally grateful. I am now embracing Emily and fully breaking free. It's taken twenty long years, but it is the most beautiful feeling in the world.

The bravest thing I ever did was continue to live when I wanted to die.

Biography:

Emily Nuttall is a trainee counsellor who's just completed her Level 3. She's an expert by experience, advisory board member for Eating Disorders, lived experience lead for the King's Transitions eating disorders youth intervention project, an inspirational speaker, trainer, and project worker, an inspiring individual who's overcome many adversities with her lived experiences of anorexia, depression, self-harm, anxiety, autism, traumas, disabilities, suicide, emotional abuse, homelessness, and family breakdowns. She works, speaks, trains, and delivers projects as an expert by experience in the areas of neurodiversity, autism, eating disorders, self-harm, suicide, disabilities, education, and trauma, with many organisations. These include the States of Guernsey Autism, Mental Health, Education and Eating Disorder Services for both children and adults; Beat, the UK eating disorders charity; Freed; Peace Pathway, Guernsey; and UK Mind; Samaritans; Grassroots Suicide Prevention; EDAC; EDCRN; Kings College, Maudsley, and other NHS trusts; CEDS; PEDS; Family Action, Autism Bedfordshire; Action for Children; Birmingham University; Bournemouth University. She also delivers projects and training independently with her Motivate the Mind business in these areas.

Emily's a co-author of 12 books, a volunteer disability sports coach and mentor with several services, communities and charities, empowering and inspiring long-lasting change.

You can connect with Emily here:

https://linktr.ee/emilyn93

Mental Health and Migration
By Jules Reynolds

'When life is hard,' said the horse, 'go softly with yourself.' — Charlie Mackesy

In order to understand the impact of migration on mental health and wellbeing, we need to be clear about who a migrant is, what the act of migration involves, and the reasons why people migrate.

Migrant: a person who is in the process of moving or has moved from their usual place of residence.

Migration: falls into two broad categories:

1. Internal — from one place to another within a state, country, or continent

2. External — from one place to another that is located in a different state, country, or continent

Motivation: there are several basic factors that motivate a migrant. These were identified by Everett Lee in 1966. He called it the 'push-pull' theory. Lee's theory is a listing of the factors that motivate a person to migrate. The 'push' factors propel a person away from their place of origin. The 'pull' factors propel a person towards their place of destination. I have modified some of the phrases used.

Push factors

Employment — minimal job opportunities; minimal training and skills

Economic — poor housing; lack of healthcare access; insolvency; low income

Ecological — natural disasters

Environmental — family links; bullying; war; poor chances of relationships

Equity — political discrimination; racial discrimination; sexual discrimination

Education — low academic achievement; high artistic abilities

Pull factors

Employment — wide range of job opportunities; improvement of training and skills

Economic — better living conditions; ease of medical care access; higher income

Ecological — attractive climates

Environmental — family links; security; stability; better chances of relationships

Equity — political impartiality; religious impartiality; sexual impartiality

Educational — improved academic success; artistic abilities recognised and valued

The process of migration has a profound and lasting influence on the social, economic, religious, political, cultural, and health aspects of a region and the people therein.

The experience of migration is a key determinant of general wellbeing and health. There are particular stresses in each phase of the migration process. Any specific psychological distress is influenced by the nature of the migration experience in which the individual is involved.

There are five identified international patterns of migration. These are:

- Short distance
- Rural to rural
- Long distance
- Rural to urban
- Urban to rural

Internal Migration

One of the major fall-out factors of the COVID-19 pandemic was that many adults realised they could do their daily work from home. Location was no longer a priority; proximity to the workplace became irrelevant. The rose-tinted allure of relocating to a 'better' place became a very powerful factor in many people's lives.

The urban to rural pattern listed above is one that is prevalent in the programming schedules of the five main broadcasting channels in the United Kingdom. TV series such as 'Escape to the Country', for example, promote the social, economic, cultural, and health benefits of living in a rural community. They polish the pastoral dream of dwelling in a rural idyll where you know your neighbours and your neighbours know you. The local pub is a thriving hub of the community, the church and its vicar provide a service of community support and, of course, it's the ideal location for those perfect social media shots of your new life. The local schools are rated 'Outstanding' by OFSTED, and your social media worthy main street boasts a post office, shop (that stocks everything you need), doctors' surgery, and dentist.

However, this public relations polish is but a very thin veneer that covers over the cracks of reality. If you want to relocate to a rural paradise, you must be prepared to encounter poor transport infrastructure, consistently weak internet connections, and frequently disrupted power supplies.

For children and young people who find themselves relocated from an urban landscape to a rural one, there is the added factor of age-appropriate schools and other educational facilities being much more than a short walk away from home. Many village primary schools have closed, and subsidised school transport has been subject to severe cuts, if not cancelled completely, by financially hard-pressed local councils.

I have worked with young people who had a daily commute of one hour to school from home and one hour from school back to home. This all took place on public transport for the vast majority of them, which meant they were subject to the variants of transport staff illness, mechanical breakdowns, road traffic accidents, and volume of traffic, in their attempt to arrive at school on time. And all of this unpredictability and stress occurred before they entered into the whirlwind that is the school environment. That one-hour commute in the morning was not conducive to preparing themselves mentally for the academic stimulation of the day. Neither was the one-hour commute in the afternoon/evening conducive to unwinding from the demands of the day and preparing for the rigours of homework.

During the 18 years of my first marriage, we migrated internally in the United Kingdom eight times. For context, my husband was employed as a Children's and Young People's Worker within a church denominational format. That means that we spent an average of twenty-seven months in each location. Whilst on paper that may seem a reasonably long period of time, when it comes to developing a sense of belonging and integration in a location, it is a very short period of time.

Research suggests that to move from the acquaintance level of friendship to becoming close friends takes over 200 hours of time and effort. Friendships cannot be forced or arranged. They must be organic in order to grow, develop, and thrive. Having the same age, gender, ethnicity, social position, and religious beliefs as someone else does not mean that you are automatically going to become friends with them.

Friendship does not just happen. It is a product of many hours spent together, engaging in mutual activities and sharing everyday conversations. Those hours are the most important factor when predicting closeness in a friendship. One of the best resources available that not only explores the mental health effects of internal migration, but also exposes the deep emotional impacts that it has on all involved, is the Pixar movie *Inside Out*. I confess that I cried when I first watched it.

The character of Riley broke my heart because she represented my daughter. The reality of our multiple migrations for her was that she attended five different primary schools between Reception Class and Year 6. Our relocations took us from locations in the West Midlands to Yorkshire, then from Yorkshire to Hertfordshire, and from

Hertfordshire to the South Coast. This move to the South Coast of the United Kingdom turned out to be the penultimate move of my first marriage. It was also the most difficult migration for my daughter.

Despite informing the local education authority in the beginning of July of our imminent arrival (we actually moved in the August) and of my daughter's need for a place in a local primary school from the beginning of the new school year in the September, it took them six weeks to sort her placement out. This resulted in her not starting at that school until the October! School uniform was then difficult to source, as all the local outlets had stopped stocking and selling specific school uniform items in mid-September. After all, what kind of parent is looking to buy school uniform in October? So, not only was my daughter the newbie — again — but she was now the late-starting newbie. Friendship groups were well established in her class, especially among the girls. For the first time within a school context, my daughter experienced bullying and social exclusion. She was eight years old.

We were always the outsiders, the newbies. When we arrived, everyone knew who we were because of the nature of my husband's employment. However, we didn't know anything about these people we were expected to become friends with. Which names matched which faces? Who was related to who? What were they expecting of us and from us? Where were we supposed to fit ourselves into in this well-established community?

External Migration

The biggest barrier that external migrants face when it comes to the issue of social integration and community cohesion is language. Speech is power, but if you cannot make yourself understood or understand those around you, then you very quickly become disenfranchised and excluded. This lack of local language skills can result in feelings of discouragement or isolation.

Understanding the importance of having adequate language skills to be able to access the same opportunities available to local language speakers is, arguably, a major motivating factor for migrants.

In my current employment, I work with secondary-aged young people who have English as an additional language. For all of them, the decision to move to the United Kingdom was not one that they made. They were brought here by the adults responsible for them.

The motivation to learn English varies widely amongst them. Some are extremely focused and see their time living here as a great opportunity to increase their academic and cultural currency. For others, however, living in the United Kingdom is a situation that they endure, and they will learn the minimum language required to get along. They will not adapt to the cultural norms around them, and they will kick against any school rules and disciplines that they encounter. Whilst the basic social components of any language can be learnt within 2-3 months, to reach the same level of academic language ability as their peers can take up to six years.

For some of these young people, there is the added ingredient of trauma to deal with. Something most of us will encounter and experience in our lives, trauma is an intense emotional response to a distressing event. The way in which it is presented, however, will vary greatly between each individual. For the young people that I work with, that distressing event is conflict.

Studies show that when migrants are unfamiliar with the language of the country that they now find themselves in, it creates barriers that prevent proper integration into that society, which in turn has a harming effect on their mental health.

Mental health affects physical health, and physical health affects mental health. The two are inseparable when it comes to overall wellbeing. While being an external migrant does not make those individuals more likely to develop mental ill health, the very fact that they are a migrant exposes them to various stress factors that will influence their mental wellbeing.

Social and psychological distress among external migrants manifests in four main areas. They are:

- Behavioural

- Cognitive

- Emotional

- Physical

Behavioural

Symptoms of behavioural distress include aggression; withdrawal; sleep disturbance; interpersonal difficulties; bed wetting; substance use.

Cognitive

Symptoms of cognitive distress include an attitude of helplessness; an acute awareness of a loss of control; boredom; overwhelming hopelessness.

Emotional

Symptoms of emotional distress include frustration; anxiety; despair; anger; grief; fear; sadness.

Physical

Symptoms of physical distress include loss of appetite; aches and pains, and bodily discomfort that cannot be medically explained.

These responses can vary widely and may change over time. And initial elation at arriving in a safe place may later give way to overwhelming grief and guilt for the places and people they have left behind.

Self-esteem is understood by psychologists as a general attitude toward the value or worth of oneself. Psychologists believe that self-esteem is social in nature. It develops along with the interactions experienced with the society around it. If the society around you is demeaning your self-worth and undermining your self-image, then your estimation of yourself will also fall. If the society around you tells you that you don't belong there and strongly advises you to 'go back home', then your sense of identity and purpose will plummet. Your low self-esteem eventually becomes visceral — that is 'deep inward feelings that are instinctive, not intellectual'.

There is an increasing body of evidence that points towards the understanding that friendships can influence everything from the strength of our immune system to the statistical chances of our dying from heart disease. Interestingly, it has also been found that once the 'buzz' of a new relationship has faded, it can often take at least one year for that friendship to become fully developed and mature.

Conclusion

So, how can you best support yourself and your children through the migration process? The acronym of CHIME, which is often used to describe the recovery process from mental ill health to mental wellness, is a useful framework.

C: Community Connections. If possible, before you move, identify groups in your new location that offer facilities and opportunities that connect with your children's current hobbies and interests. Also, try to arrange a visit to your child's new school before you move. At the very least, look on their website together so that you all become familiar with the school facilities, their declared ethos, and academic focus. Discover details about your new location and discuss them together.

H: **Hope.** Where there is life, there is hope. Having aspirations for the future helps us to think positively about life. Hope is not a vague wish but a solid belief that what we cannot yet see — those new friendships, for example — actually already exist. Future me will grow to love my new community, even if present me is apprehensive and a little scared.

I: Identity. Instil a pride in your children about how they look, how they speak, and the life experiences they have already had. My daughter is proud of her family roots and her genetic inheritance. However, as she grew older, she realised that in order to be able to integrate herself more quickly in each new location, she needed to be able to match the speaking patterns of her new peers. She didn't end up sounding like a long-term local, but neither did she sound like a total outsider. This was a valuable survival skill for her.

M: **Meaning.** Many factors contribute to the feeling of having a meaningful life. These can include roles within our community; academic goals in education; our place within our family unit. Ensure that these factors are ones that your children can take ownership of. It has to be their dreams that they are chasing, not yours.

E: **Empowerment.** Taking responsibility for and control of aspects of our lives is empowering. Let your child pack their personal belongings. Talk about the specialness or significance of each item for them and the memories connected to each one. Talk about making new memories and wonder out loud who else will be part of them.

Above all else, **BE HONEST!** Make sure that your child understands that you have hopes and fears about the move, just as they do. Be honest about why you are moving and why you have chosen the new location. Answer all questions and do not dismiss their concerns as irrelevant or irritating. Listen to learn, not lecture.

Preparation will not prevent disappointments occurring. Planning will not mitigate against all circumstances.

But honesty will ensure that you arrive and stay together.

Dedication:

Ariella and Pete — fellow migrants on this journey of life.

Biography:

Jules Reynolds has the heart of a teacher. She loves to pass on her passion and enthusiasm for language and all things etymological to others. Her adult life has always involved working with children and young people. At the age of 49 she decided to begin an undergraduate course in Speech and Language Therapy at university, graduating in 2021.

Jules's current employment is as a Higher-Level Teaching Assistant for students with English as an Additional Language.

Married with one grown-up daughter, Jules has personal experience of poor mental health, including bouts of nervous exhaustion and clinical depression.

A self-confessed word nerd, music also features strongly in her life — listening, playing, and composing.

You can connect with Jules here:
https://linktr.ee/julesyaffa

Exploring Neurodiversity for Your Child
By Emma Sails

'Neurodiversity isn't actually about having a specific, catalogued "defect" that the psychiatric establishment has an explanation for. It's about being different in a way others struggle to understand or refuse to accept.'
Quote from Judy Singer, used by Devon Price in Unmasking Autism: Discovering the New Faces of Neurodiversity.

When I found out about my own ADHD (Attention Deficit Hyperactivity Disorder) and autism, I could start to see my childhood through a completely different lens than I'd been able to before. I could see that a lot of the labels I was given or names I had been called as a child were a result of neurodivergent traits, but by the time I knew this they had completely shaped my identity. There was a lot of resentment to process about how different things could have been for me as a child if I had known, but of course that was impossible at the time; the research simply hadn't been done. Girls didn't have ADHD when I was growing up, and nobody knew how autism could present in girls (and some boys), or for the most part even what neurodivergent masking (the ability to mirror what society expects of you so that you can seem to fit in, regardless of how you feel internally) was.

Thankfully, there is a lot more information out there now about what neurodivergence is and how it impacts us. Parents can learn about different kinds of neurodivergence and what it can look like, so that they can teach and support their children, which can ultimately prevent the negative labels from becoming a part of their identity.

However, we often have such strong mental images associated with conditions such as autism and ADHD that it can be very difficult to consider that our child may be impacted by neurodivergence. It's common to worry that a diagnosis of these conditions gives our children a label that will be like a prison sentence for them, and it's also common to look at our children and find it very difficult to consider that they may have a disability, invisible or not.

In this chapter I would like to ease some of the concern that contemplating neurodivergence as an explanation for how your child is struggling can provoke. To start with, I will explain a little about the facts of what neurodiversity — and neurodivergence — actually is.

What is neurodiversity?

Neurodiversity is a word that was coined by Judy Singer to describe the differences in how brains work throughout the human race... and it includes EVERYONE. All of humanity is neurodiverse, and no two brains are the same. That's why you may hear people saying, 'Everyone is a little bit ADHD/autistic.' No, everyone is human.

What we need to explore, though, are the sub-categories within neurodiversity which, to simplify, are:

Neurotypical: anyone who fits into 'the norm' of thinking patterns — anyone whose life is not significantly impacted by their brain working 'differently'. The majority of people are classed as neurotypical, and society has been built to the neurotypical way of communicating and approaching things.

Neurodivergent: anyone differing in mental or neurological function from what is considered typical or 'normal'. To simplify, if you have multiple neurodivergent traits (not all traits, because nobody has every trait they read about) impacting you every day, then it is completely ok to refer to yourself, or think of yourself, as neurodivergent.

The 'symptoms' of neurodivergence are known as traits, because a symptom is something indicative of a disease, whereas a trait describes a part or characteristic of someone's personality. There are a lot of neurodivergent traits, and most of them can be experienced by both neurotypical and neurodivergent people. (I have traits lists available to download. Check out my biography for details.)

For example, procrastination is something that everyone experiences; everyone puts things off sometimes, and everyone can't do things that they should be able to do sometimes. However, when someone is procrastinating to the point where they have to work overnight to meet a deadline, or where things regularly don't get done and it impacts their life (almost) daily, then that's where it becomes a neurodivergent trait.

So, if there are traits of neurodivergence that are impacting your child's life on a daily basis, that are happening consistently, and that are stopping them from achieving what they want to or holding them back in any way, then that is where it's useful to consider getting some support and exploring potential neurodivergence.

As the quote says at the top of this chapter, a lot of the issues around neurodivergence stem from a lack of understanding and acceptance. If we can teach people how neurodivergent brains work, and tweak the way that schools and employers communicate, it would be so much easier for the neurodivergent community. If schools approached teaching as if every child was neurodivergent, it would not be harmful to neurotypical children, but neurodivergent children would benefit enormously.

Crossovers between conditions

There are a LOT of crossovers between different neurodivergent conditions. With neurodivergence, the diagnosis is based on which set of traits someone presents with most predominantly, and until quite recently it was said that people could only be diagnosed with one of these conditions. However, as research has gone on, it has been discovered that, as an example, around 50-70% of autistic people also have ADHD. When you flip that, around 40% of people with ADHD are also autistic. Those are very high numbers. ADHD and autism are two of the most comorbid conditions there are, and to further complicate things in the diagnosis of AuDHD (both ADHD and autism) medical professionals must take into account that the traits of either one can sometimes hide the traits of the other. For example, the need for routine in autism can change how the chaos associated with ADHD presents outwardly.

If you look at the table below, I have listed some of the most common traits for the five most commonly diagnosed neurodivergent conditions. If you search online for any of these conditions, you would find these things as a list of traits, but what you wouldn't necessarily see are the overlaps.

Condition	Traits	Initial Crossovers
Autism (ASD)	• Communication issues • Difficulty (or exhaustion from) socialising • Repetitive behaviour • Need for routine	• Inability to do daily tasks (e.g. potential poor hygiene) • Stimming (vocal or physical)
ADHD	• Impulsivity • Hyperactivity (either physical, mental, or both) • Interrupting / seeming rude • Time blindness	
Dyslexia	• Delay with spoken and/or written language • Uses anagrams of words • Confusion ordering letters	• Issues with sequencing and order (days of the week, etc)
Dyscalculia	• Issues identifying number groups and ordering numbers • Struggle to identify shapes	
Dyspraxia	• Accident prone • Co-ordination issues (may be slow to walk/run or struggle with agility) • Issues using both hands together (e.g. tying laces, using cutlery)	
ALL Neurodivergent conditions can result in... • Resistance to doing work/schoolwork/school refusal • Procrastination/leaving things to the last minute • Poor concentration/focus/difficulty following instructions • Emotional sensitivity/anxiety • Sensory issues with light/sound/taste, etc		

Examples of some other diagnosable neurodivergent conditions which may also crossover with the above are: Down Syndrome, Tourette Syndrome, Auditory Processing Disorder, Sensory Processing Disorder, and more. Other neurological conditions such as epilepsy, DiGeorge Syndrome, and Williams Syndrome often co-occur, along with mental health conditions such as anxiety, bipolar disorder, and Obsessive-Compulsive Disorder (OCD).

To finish off this section, please know that until you have spoken to a medical professional about your child's specific struggles, it is completely ok to say that you suspect they are neurodivergent without defining how. As I mentioned above, every brain is unique, and everyone presents in a slightly different way. All we are doing by looking into a diagnosis is helping to categorise the traits in a way that makes it as easy as possible to support your child.

What's in a label?

My response to anyone who asks why you would want to give your child a label, or diagnosis, is to point out the many labels that so many late diagnosed neurodivergent people — myself included — identify with. An undiagnosed neurodivergent child may already be labelled as weird, useless, idiotic, stupid, awkward, lazy, gullible, boring, or many other negative things that we do not want our children to feel about themselves. Knowledge about neurodivergence and/or having a diagnosis is an explanation, not a label.

To provide some context on this, I'm going to delve into my own childhood a little and explain how different neurodivergent traits presented in my childhood and caused the above negative labels to stick.

I will talk more about rejection sensitivity later, but that was the reason I spent my teenage years hidden behind someone else. I rarely showed my personality or shared what I was interested in with peers for fear of being judged or rejected. I was very shy and quiet at school, but for most of it I was a model student — one of the top students in class and overachieving in most areas. I was also motivated by proving people wrong or proving myself to be capable; if anyone told me I would be unable to achieve something, I would go out of my way to achieve it.

On the flip side, I had awful meltdowns at home. I had a very difficult relationship with my dad while I was younger as a result, because I slammed doors, I screamed, I shouted, and nobody at school would have guessed any of that was happening. When I wasn't having a meltdown, most of the time at home was spent hidden in my room, doing my jigsaw and listening to music, which I now understand was my recharge time.

I was badly bullied at school. The interesting thing about bullying is that often both the bully and the bullied are neurodivergent but presenting in different ways. You've got one child going into fight mode and taking over, and one child who is going into flight or fawn and curling up and enabling the bully to fight. It's difficult for children who don't know how to communicate or how to make themselves feel strong, heard, and in control, which is basically what they're trying to do when they're bullying. However, for the child who's being bullied, it's utterly horrific.

I missed social cues and lacked in social awareness, often not understanding what other children were trying to communicate. I was very trusting and often misunderstood jokes; if somebody said something to me, I took them at face value, which resulted in leaving myself open to mockery from both my friends and from others.

I had sensory issues around food, and around light. I had to eat my lunch in a particular order and had the same thing to eat most days. I was very overwhelmed and anxious a lot of the time and was often very defensive when anyone questioned my reasons for doing things or commented on what I was doing.

That is just a little touch on my story. I could write more, but this is just from my perspective and gives one version of how neurodivergence presents. As the saying goes, if you meet one neurodivergent person, you've met one neurodivergent person; there are a lot of different ways neurodivergence presents in both children and in adults.

Three key areas in which neurodivergence can impact behaviour

1. Rejection Sensitivity (sometimes Rejection Sensitive Dysphoria, or RSD)

Rejection sensitivity is arguably the biggest influence on neurodivergent behaviour in both adults and children. For children with RSD, emotional rejection or perceived rejection presents as physical pain in the body, which often causes a knee-jerk reaction. A lot of our behaviour stems from trying to avoid that physical pain. Without RSD, rejection is still felt strongly due to the need to fit in and the feeling of being 'different' to your peers.

Rejection sensitivity can cause lashing out or being 'over-sensitive'. If a child has done something wrong, when RSD is involved even something that may seem tiny to outsiders becomes a huge deal, due to the feeling of pain. It can cause running away (from school or from home) or lashing out; essentially, this feeling may put your child into a fight or flight response.

Refusal to do or hand in schoolwork is another presentation of rejection sensitivity; getting a bad mark or failing is a form of rejection, so sometimes it may seem easier for your child to just not to do the work. Similarly with refusing to go to school. If there's potential conflict there, whether it's with teachers or with their peers, avoiding school is avoiding rejection.

People pleasing is also a reaction to rejection sensitivity. If we make ourselves needed, we are theoretically less likely to be rejected, so children struggling with rejection sensitivity may seem easily led or struggle to say no for fear of the consequences. You may notice that your child is like a chameleon and seems to be a different person depending on which group of friends they're with. This is a form of people pleasing and, again, is to avoid rejection.

The best thing to help with rejection sensitivity is constant reassurance that it's ok to make mistakes, that your child is loved and valued as they are, and that they are safe.

2. Pathological Demand Avoidance (PDA)

PDA is essentially finding it difficult or sometimes impossible to comply with requests or expectations, and often social demands. Generally, behaviour associated with PDA is worse when a child is overwhelmed or over-stimulated, so that even smaller tasks (such as hanging their coat up or, with younger children, dressing themselves) can become impossible. In school there are so many demands put on our children that often when they get home, they just can't deal with any more. Especially in the case of children who mask (or hide) their neurodivergence at school.

Basic hygiene and self-care are sometimes a struggle with PDA, because there is often little to no enjoyment in looking after ourselves, and it can get in the way of more exciting things or special interests, etc.

You may find that you can repeatedly ask your child to do something, and they just ignore you completely or they change the subject to something else entirely to avoid any focus on the task they haven't done. (They may have wanted to do it, but it's just been too much and now they're trying to distract you, because if you get angry it then triggers rejection sensitivity.)

It may be useful to try giving your child an option between two things, e.g. 'Would you rather do X or Y?' Also change the 'can you?' to 'it would really help me if you could...'. Try and phrase things so that they don't sound like demands.

Another way that PDA presents is with a struggle to respect figures of authority or issues with hierarchy, for example teachers. Neurodivergent children will often socialise or speak to adults rather than other children. As an example, if they go to a birthday party or a school function, they're likely to help set the chairs out and put things away rather than socialise with the other children; it is a way to be there and take part, but it's less risky. Adults are generally less likely to reject you than other children.

3. The pressure to appear neurotypical

Society is not built for neurodivergent brains, and a lot of neurodivergent children put a massive amount of energy into masking (to present how they think people want to see them).

If your child is completely fine at school and then exploding at home, this could well be because they are masking, which is exhausting, and then coming home to their safe space and letting go of the mask. That results in extra energy to release, overwhelm that has built up, leaving a child incredibly sensitive to anything outside of what they are expecting from that home environment.

The higher the level of masking in children, the bigger the risk of mental health struggles and potential burnout in their teens, going on to potential Complex Post-Traumatic Stress Disorder (CPTSD) later in life. Again, reassuring our children that they are brilliant as they are and that they don't need to hide themselves from their peers, is vital. The safer they feel in their home environments and the more they are encouraged to be themselves the better.

Next Steps

Note: this advice is for people based in the UK.

If you have read this and feel that there is a good chance your child is neurodivergent, the first step is to reach out to their teacher and to the SENDCO (sometimes SENCO, meaning Special Educational Needs and/or Disabilities Co-ordinator) at their school. Often teachers have not had any training about neurodiversity or communicating with neurodivergent children, so ensure that you include the SENDCO in all correspondence if possible. The details of the school SENDCO should be publicised on their website.

The school should then arrange to meet with you and discuss the areas in which your child is struggling, and then start a process of observation. After this process, the school will decide whether there is a case to send to CAMHS (Child and Adolescent Mental Health Services), to move towards a neurodivergent diagnosis, and to set up an EHCP (Education, Health and Care Plan) to support your child in school. If you have any problems progressing your case with school, look up your local SENDIASS (Special Educational Needs and Disabilities Information, Advice and Support Service) who will be able to provide you with free, impartial advice on moving forward.

Often, schools are underfunded, and diagnosis takes a long time, therefore it's important to do your own research into how best to support your child. There are a lot of Facebook Support Groups, and there will always be other parents in your area who are going through the same thing with their child. It can feel like a very lonely fight to get your child the support they need, but it is a fight that is worth having.

Finally, it's important to note that you only know what you know. Parents often feel a lot of guilt when going through this with their children, but please acknowledge how hard you are trying. You are doing the best for them that you know how to do, and the fact that you are reading this book proves that.

Dedication:

Dedicated to Tyler, who is my motivation for learning about any of this in the first place.

Biography:

Emma Sails is an ICF-accredited life coach who has done a significant amount of neurodivergent specific training. She works as a coach and mentor with neurodivergent adults and parents of neurodivergent children, to help them understand and accept how neurodivergence impacts their lives, and what they can do to stop it from holding them back.

When Emma found out about her own neurodivergence aged 35, everything changed for her. She had just come through a battle with post-natal depression and ended her marriage, and she was on a mission to figure out what she wanted in life and how to be the best role model for her son.

Diagnosis of ADHD and autism gave her an answer to a lot of the struggles she'd faced throughout her life, and she set out to spread awareness and help others on the same journey. Emma's ultimate goal is to ensure that future generations of neurodivergent children don't have to go through the same trials growing up as her generation did.

You can connect with Emma here:

https://linktr.ee/EmmaSailsCoaching

Other Collaborative Projects
By Cassie Swift

Navigating Anxiety with Children & Teens

Navigating Anxiety with Children & Teens shares advice, strategies and real life examples from a collaboration of 13 experts in their field. It focuses on ways to navigate different forms of anxiety, from how we frame the term 'anxiety', to dealing with terminal illness, to the very real mum guilt. The aim is to aid you in supporting our younger generation as well as reminding you that you are not alone - there are many people available to help you on this journey.

The chapters share real life stories and activities on dealing with the many different forms of anxiety our young people face. With the added bonus of audio links, it also means it is accessible for everyone to benefit from. If you are struggling to navigate anxiety then this book is a must read for you.

You can order your copy here: https://bit.ly/NAWCAT

Hold on to Hope

Hold on to Hope brings together 19 amazing women who are sharing their stories to overcoming challenges they have faced. This book aims to share that, by holding on to hope, you will be able to overcome any situation you are faced with! The women in this book have found their healing and peace by sharing their stories – one day this could be you too.

You can order your copy here: https://bit.ly/holdhope

What I Wish I Had Heard

What I Wish I Had Heard: Stories From Our Inner Child, brings together ten incredible and inspirational women in a powerful and heartfelt collaboration where they share stories from their inner child. They have had to dig deep to connect with the younger versions of themselves to present you their stories about feelings of worth, bullying, abuse, and so many more. Not only has this brought them healing and peace, but we hope that it will introduce you to just how powerful the concept of the inner child is and may even start you on your own healing journey.

The chapters share stories of self discovery and deep connection as well as activities the authors themselves have used to aid their healing. With the added bonus of audio links, it also means it is accessible for everyone to benefit from.

Remember, you are not alone or broken, healing is open to everyone including YOU!

You can order your copy here: https://bit.ly/WIWIHH

www.ingramcontent.com/pod-product-compliance
Lightning Source LLC
Chambersburg PA
CBHW061207070526
44583CB00025B/3149